WELCOME TO THE JUNGLE

A Guide to Surviving and Thriving in Corporate America While Creating Your Dream Life

Inspired by My Journey from the Reception Desk to the C-Suite

Teena Hostovich

WELCOME TO THE JUNGLE
A Guide to Surviving and Thriving in Corporate America While Creating Your
Dream Life
Inspired by my Journey From the Reception Desk to the C-Suite

Teena Hostovich

For more information: TeenaHostovich@gmail.com
PAPERBACK ISBN: 978-1-962280-05-1
EBOOK ISBN: 978-1-962280-04-4

Get your FREE resources here:

Visit www.TeenaHostovich.com/book

OR

scan the QR code below

Before you start, I want to thank you for picking up *Welcome to the Jungle* and being interested in reading and learning from my journey, from reception desk to C-suite! As a thank-you, when you visit the link or scan the QR code above, you'll receive:

- "GET READY TO ROCK THE INTERVIEW" CHECKLIST
- "DISCOVER YOUR TRUE WHY" CHECKLIST
- VIP EARLY ACCESS TO MY NEXT BOOK, RELEASED IN 2025

PRAISE FOR WELCOME TO THE JUNGLE

"Teena Hostovich is a proven and passionate leader whose wisdom and practical advice will benefit anyone starting a career in business."

—Secretary Hillary Rodham Clinton

"Teena Hostovich is a trailblazer and the most civically engaged leader and the most pay-it-forward person that I know. She has helped legions of people and students navigate their careers and gives selflessly to help guide and mentor others. This book is a Must-Read."

—Dean Geoffrey Garrett, University of Southern California, Marshall School of Business

"Teena Hostovich is an accomplished thought leader who has imparted actionable wisdom to California's dreamers and doers over decades. Her incisive book is not just useful for aspiring entrepreneurs and business leaders, but essential."

—Governor Gavin Newsom, California

For Doug and Michael, Always and Forever

TABLE OF CONTENTS

Introduction

Being murdered began to seem like both a possibility and the better option.

Right around the time I realized this, I was choking on the blood filling my mouth. Things were bad and appeared to be getting worse quickly. When I got punched full force in the jaw (which, if you never have been, trust me—hurts like you can't believe!) and called a creative slew of obscenities, I knew things were officially out of control.

Shall we start at the beginning?

It was an innocent enough request. I was asked to meet a client of my boss's boss's boss (from the New York office) for a drink at the Los Angeles Country Club to discuss a new business opportunity involving . . . me. It was my first real chance to demonstrate I could perform at a more senior level, so I was both excited and nervous. It felt like it could be my shot, or at least a first step.

My visits to LACC back then were beyond rare, and being asked to do anything for anyone on the firm's private board of directors was almost like a solar eclipse, a blue moon, or some other rare event. Honestly, it didn't occur to me (like so many things back then) to ask, "Why me?"

It wouldn't have mattered. To refuse was to show incredible disrespect and lack of appreciation for the opportunity, so I never even considered it. This was a very different time; you didn't question what you were asked to do or you would be asked to leave the firm—permanently. But I would never have thought to fear for my safety.

Off I went. Working in Century City, it was a fairly easy walk to the Club for my then twenty-year-old self, so I walked over. I left my poor little car proudly sitting in a spot at the very bottom of the lot for the two towers of Century Park East—a structure that has a lot in common with the Matterhorn and Space Mountain at Disneyland. Moving your car during normal business hours was a bit of a risk, but had I known . . .

I'm getting ahead of myself. When I arrived, I did notice this client was a singularly unattractive man. (If I were a less kind person, I might even describe him as a troll or an extra from *Lord of the Rings*. One of the orcs, not the hot Orlando Bloom elves.) He spent the evening talking about himself, his money, his car (a Porsche, as a matter of interest), his unusual grooming habits (you don't want to know!), and his plane. I'd never met anyone at this point in my life who owned a plane, let alone multiple houses in fabulous cities. He seemed to do interesting work; I could see a connection between that work and his financial security. But I felt more than a bit out of my depth, honestly. Why was he so intent on meeting me? I couldn't afford to shop anywhere appropriate, my old car was held together by duct tape, and my position was very junior. But since I was raised by a Southern mom and manners are part of my DNA, I didn't want to hurt his feelings. This might be a good time to point out that many young women have actually died of politeness.

I did, however, want to go home after about fifteen minutes; two hours went by. Searching for any excuse, even a lame one, I actually said, "I need to get home before *Mork and Mindy* comes on." (Loved Robin Williams, and these were pre-streaming and recording days). He looked at me like I'd sprouted another head. He said, "Your boss said you were a nice and very accommodating girl! That's a lie!" I began to feel a strong sense of unease, a tingle of dread up my spine. This wasn't going anywhere good. As far as opportunities go, this was NOT going to be one, at least not one to do anything I would want to do.

I was completely inarticulate and muttered some garbled phrase. The unease was morphing into actual fear.

He insisted on driving me back to my car at the Matterhorn. It was getting dark, and traffic was going to be a challenge since I lived far from Century City. I very reluctantly agreed, with my brain screaming, "What is the matter with you, moron? RUN!" In my defense, I was young, and although I'd lived overseas and wasn't totally clueless, I was hopeless with confrontation.

The nerve-racking drive took five uncomfortably silent but uneventful minutes. Creepy horror film music was filling my head.

He parked next to my shabby little car in the bowels of the parking structure, turned off his engine, and looked at me. I was expecting the semi-polite fumble and deftly avoided the good-night kiss he was clearly expecting. He pushed the locks, simultaneously pulled back his right fist, and punched me straight in the jaw. (Did I mention, it REALLY hurt?)

I saw stars for real. I think I might have blacked out for a moment because the next thing I knew, he was tying my hands to the gearshift. Fortunately (odd choice of words for the moment, but . . .), he WAS a moron and used a bungee cord. Yep, a bungee cord! For those who haven't had any bungee cord experiences (no jumping off bridges or attempted kidnappings, for example), the cord gives. And while he might have been counting on the blow to disable me, I was young and strong, so I was still conscious. With consciousness came full-on fear.

When he moved in to tell me he was taking me to his plane at LAX (these were the days BEFORE all the documentaries and conversations; we didn't know much about trafficking), he just couldn't resist leaning in, all drooly and repulsive, for a kiss. I took an adrenaline-fueled chance, using the give in the cord to lock my fingers together, form a tight fist, and push upward at that exact moment to break his nose. Blood gushed everywhere. And I mean EVERYWHERE—the windshield, my blouse, dripping down his face and mine (and there was still my blood-filled mouth).

I reached across him to disable the locks and ran to my car to shouts of, "I'm going to kill you right now, you ungrateful, stupid bitch!" I drove out of the garage like the car was on fire, didn't use my exit card, drove through the barricade (destroying it), and raced home.

About a mile from my parents' house, I stopped at a gas station to wipe the blood off myself, rinse out my mouth, and discover the missing tooth. I snuck in the house so as not to wake my mom and dad, collapsed on the bed, and never dealt with that trauma until recently.

Afterward, I was called into the office of the "big boss" and threatened with termination. I had to think quickly, be clever but pleading, and grovel to get myself out of being fired for fending off a would-be kidnapper and God knows what else.

Lesson noted.

This was a moment in time over forty years ago that illustrates the dark corners of the past in the gender power dynamic. I share it not to elicit sympathy or hold anyone accountable (those who would be are actually dead, so in a way . . .) but to take you back to a time in my life when I realized that rules and guidelines were merely "suggestions" to those in control. We saw the power of the #MeToo movement, which came after years of normalizing abuse in the workplace. And trafficking and exploitation of young people continues; Jeffrey Epstein was on trial for trafficking as recently as 2019 at the time of his death. I realized way back at the time of this incident that there were many parallels between my life in a large global organization and the actual jungle; the animals were slightly different, but perils abound in both.

My name is Teena Hostovich. I am, first and foremost, a survivor. I've survived cancer, a stroke, the early loss of both parents, personal violence, depression, and a veritable cornucopia of chaos. And I'm still here, feeling beyond blessed and a bit amazed. I am a senior leader of a global organization, and I am also a wife, mother, family member, and friend.

This book is my way to inspire and empower you to conquer the obstacles in your path and to achieve nothing less than your dreams. Please read on for tales of determination and resilience, along with unexpected and unimaginable events.

These "adventures" are what I've learned over the past four decades. They may shock you. They may motivate you. But I hope they'll genuinely help you and change your life just a little. I'm filled with gratitude that you've chosen to read this book, and I promise that I'm here to help you.

Please remember that anything is possible in the pursuit of your own path to success. This book will take you from Day 1 of your first "real" job or from Today on the job you're already in, to an outcome that will position you well for a successful career and a life of meaning and joy.

I'll always be honest with you, and I'll be the kind of friend to you that I want to have. I've tried to accept responsibility for the times I caused my own suffering or made terrible decisions, staying clear-eyed and self-aware. My own journey has been anything but a straight line or a linear, logical path. It's been a great ride (I know I'm dating myself here), like the old E tickets from Disneyland that allowed you to ride THE coolest rides. I know there are more journeys—safaris, if you will—ahead.

During the pandemic, I had both cancer and a stroke, twelve months apart. Having almost died twice and gotten closer to the end of my career than the beginning, I was searching for my purpose anew. It's been quite a process. My deepest hope is that by reading my story, you'll come to believe in yourself even more and find actual tools you can use. I want to show you that you can be you and still succeed. That you're brave. Special. A shining star. And that you own every beautiful moment you create.

Because of my own personal experience, I write from the perspective of a woman in business. That doesn't mean that I intend to exclude men from my advice and thoughts. I'm the mother of a young man, and I've observed that the current generation of young men are struggling to find their place in a new world order. I've always believed that men and women (however you identify, and I don't judge) working together make the impossible possible.

David Bowie said, "Aging is the extraordinary process whereby you become the person you always should have been."[1]

Mr. Bowie inspired me in his search for his true self, and I feel that I'm finally at a place that's more aligned with the person I was meant to be, were it not for circumstances and people that derailed me. Some of the circumstances were beyond my control, including rules imposed by the accepted social order of the times I grew up in, as well as my background and unconventional education. Some of the blame for my derailment belongs solely at my feet. I allowed myself to create, at times, a pattern of self-destructive behavior through my own bad decisions, which gave some of my power over to others.

I'll share my pain with you because I want to spare you some of that same pain and accelerate your becoming the incredible person you ARE meant to be.

Right now, I want to truly connect with the person I was on my way to becoming before life trampled me a bit. I'm finally *almost* that person. As I've confronted my own mortality, I'd come to view her, that person, as a sibling in another country or even in another star system—just outside of my grasp.

This book is one of my first steps on that journey to reclaiming myself. I'm so very lucky to have your companionship as we explore what it means to create your ACTUAL best life. You don't have to lose your

---

1. Matt Hogan, "David Bowie on Aging Being an Extraordinary Process," MoveMe Quotes, January 8, 2021, https://movemequotes.com/beyond-the-quote-7/.

true self; you can be the person you're meant to be, even if you lose your way at times. Time and your own instincts will tell you what to do. As you look at your personal experiences to this point, you'll find some of the skills you seek to build or expand.

You have a unique set of gifts that only you possess in that combination. On days when you feel like a failure (still happens to me ALL the time), keep your "why" firmly in the front of your mind. It reveals your true purpose and what will allow you to feel fulfilled.

I recently learned that we can benefit from reflecting on what's most meaningful and precious to us by asking ourselves, "What do I most fear?" Your answer helps you better identify and understand what your deepest values are because it can also be asked as, "What do I most fear losing?" You don't fear the loss of what's not important to you. It's been established that one of the major regrets of those who are weeks from the end of their lives is that they never had the courage to live the life they wanted or were meant to have. Fear got in the way. It's continually important to always be honest, painfully so, with yourself. No one else knows your most private thoughts, hopes, dreams, and fears. If you continue to deny any of these or repress them (and we all do somewhat for super painful stuff; our minds allow us to process trauma at our own rate to accept and heal), you will NOT be able to create your dream life. You must be open to admitting, analyzing, and addressing your fears and weaknesses as well as your strengths and purpose; you'll have a happier life. I promise!

Remember that you're starting a new chapter in the book of your life. It may turn out to be the best time of your life, or you may learn some hard lessons. It may be amazing for three years or five years, but then it may be time to have a new adventure. Or it can be the seeds of a beautiful garden that you'll build where you are.

I had other ideas about what I wanted to do in my life that didn't involve being a business executive or a part of corporate America. I was in a band in middle school and high school (the drummer, always the coolest role!). We even did a demo album. When I finally arrived at the University of Southern California (USC), I wanted to be a filmmaker. None of that resulted in viable career options. However, I've found other ways to make life a grand adventure.

Through building a business career, I've been able to connect to other things that interest and motivate me, and frankly, make me happy and allow me to (I hope!) make a difference.

Each step of the way for every goal I ever had or stated, I was told there was either a 0 percent or less than 10 percent chance of my succeeding. I'll take a 10 percent chance any day; I've made it work for me. Don't let other people decide what YOU can or can't achieve. They just don't know. They can truly judge only themselves and their capabilities, not yours. If you want to achieve something badly enough, the only way there's a zero chance is if you do nothing.

Along the way, I've worked for three presidents of the United States so far in various capacities (Clinton, Obama, and Biden), and I've had a chance to be part of transformative conversations and legislation. My lifelong passions for the arts, education, history, health equity, the rights of the voiceless, and political activism have helped me tremendously in deepening both my business and personal connections and finding more meaning in my own life. Those connections form lasting relationships, which I find to be the magic ingredient of life.

I've also been able to participate in truly amazing events and meaningful things, as YOU will when your purpose aligns with your career and your life. These experiences have sustained me through many difficult situations and challenges. You can link your passions and interests to your chosen career or even your early "starter" jobs. As time goes on, your passions may change, and they may bloom and grow. And they'll give you the priceless gift of knowing you made a difference and fulfilled your purpose.

Closely related to this concept is "Who am I?" The person you are today isn't the person you'll be in five years, ten years, or more. As we grow, we learn and adapt. Your "why" ultimately informs your "who." There isn't another YOU in all the world. If you doubt the power of one, I ask you to consider the impact of just the following people (there are so many incredible humans to choose from): Winston Churchill, Volodymyr Zelensky, Nelson Mandela, Bill and Hillary Clinton, and Taylor Swift.

Brace yourself, baby! And welcome to the jungle! (Or, as it's more commonly described, corporate America.) The animals are wild, weapons are mandatory, you're going to develop survival skills you can't imagine, and blood sport isn't always a metaphor.

Chapter 1

"We Got Fun and Games":

Where on earth do you start? My advice at the beginning of your safari is to "start as you mean to go on," an old adage still having great relevance. It means to approach everything deliberately and consistently, do something well, and keep doing it. Be intentional. There's tremendous value in the way you prepare for your interview and study up on corporate culture well before your first day in the office. Think of this as doing research for a momentous trip to a long-dreamt-of place. You may look at maps, key sights, history, YouTube, or travel blogs.

My childhood helped prepare me for the road ahead in ways I would never have imagined. Growing up in a very diverse, working-class area of Los Angeles, I had experiences that many today are nostalgic for—neighborhood block parties, chatting over the fence, and shared gossip and meals. Many of our neighbors were immigrants and East Coast transplants, and my interactions with them built on an existing appreciation I had for many cultures. It also gave me early exposure to the idea that you could move across the country, choose where to build a future (even without much money), and start fresh.

But school, even elementary and middle school, could be a little rough, to put it mildly. It was the sixties and seventies—a time of progress in America but also a time of social unrest, protests, and violence. In our area, we had some gang activity, school violence, and the possibility of a stabbing or beatdown (we weren't yet at the shocking and sad situation that exists today with gun violence in schools). Because of the scope of the diversity, there were many benefits but also some inevitable tension. I was already very much "other." By middle school, I was a target for a variety of reasons (which remain a mystery to me). I was challenged to active physical fights with fists, hairpulling, razor blades, knives, and other assorted weaponry. Several girls spent time in the ER following these incidents, but we would never dream of involving any adult. And I had no illusions of being up to the task of winning in any sort of combat.

During this time, I was inspired by the story of Scheherazade, the narrator of *One Thousand and One Nights*, a collection of Middle Eastern folktales. In the story, King Shahryar, after discovering the infidelity of his first wife and in the manner of generations of imperious male rulers, executed her. He then resolved that he would marry a new virgin every day and have her beheaded the next—as one does—before she could betray him. When he ran out of "suitable" virgins—having, you know, murdered them all—Scheherazade offered to marry him against her loving father's wishes. She was a star among all her peers: extremely well-read, witty, and one hell of a storyteller by all accounts.

Scheherazade asked the king for a final favor—could she have her sister join her for a farewell story? As she told the story so beautifully, the king lay awake, listening with awe and admiration. She stopped in the middle, and he insisted that she finish. But she said that since it was already daylight, it was too late. He spared her life for the next night, and she continued the story the next, and the next, and so on. After a thousand and one nights and one thousand stories, King Shahryar had fallen madly in love with her, spared her life, and made her his queen. I view this as successfully brokering the ultimate deal under difficult circumstances.

Taking my cue from desperation and literature, I began a small story circle at recess (a time of great peril, as may be recalled by others of my generation) and began a story without an end. I would just keep it going, introducing new complications, twists, and turns. Each day, the circle of listeners grew larger and larger, and the girls who were initially the most hostile and the scariest joined in the first week. Several months later, they asked me to be the unofficial "school storyteller," and I was safe for the duration. This was my introduction to the power of story, persuasion, and creativity in combination, and I've survived on these skills ever since.

The point of my little story is that YOU know things you don't yet realize will help you tremendously and possibly save your life, metaphorically or for real. The unique experiences you've had have already shaped you in some ways and bestowed gifts upon you, even if it's not obvious. Discovering those gifts and how best to use them will take time, along with being open and genuinely thoughtful throughout your life. Trust your instincts; they are right more often than you can possibly imagine. It's a gift we are all born with, and you ignore it at your peril.

Job Quest: Where Do I Start?

One of the most important decisions you can make is where to work. Finding where we belong and where we're happy is one of the most important things we ever do. You'll change and evolve, but you need to find the first destination. You'll get it wrong, possibly, in the beginning.

Unlike in my early days, there's no longer any stigma in having had several jobs, and it can be positive. Do get into the discipline of looking for the ultimate situation, even if it takes a few years or a few tries to get there. By that, I mean be clear with yourself about what an ideal career looks like to you. Break it down into its components (flexible schedule, travel, challenging work, great colleagues, free food, whatever your Nirvana is), and work toward finding or achieving your ideal. **I have a checklist that you can sign up for at the beginning of the book to help you with that analysis.**

There are many ways to find a job now that didn't exist when I was starting my own search. Online job posts have absolutely and undeniably been a game changer, and there are several avenues to pursue there. But one of the best ways—was then, still is—is through your own contacts, whether they be friends, family, contacts from school, companies you did an internship with, or neighbors. You know, the old-fashioned human connection way. My mother helped me get my first job through people she knew, and even though she was gone too soon and too young, she impacted the rest of my life by helping me with that oh-so-important first step. I'm comforted by that daily.

The reality is that, however you get your first job, you've begun to create the rest of your life. It will take time and personal growth to find your purpose, and there are aspects of corporate or organizational behavior that feel more like a game than a step toward making an impact. Remember this to keep your sanity.

I started my safari (continuing our metaphor) as a receptionist at a small insurance brokerage firm that worked with companies based in Japan and Asia, hired for my "Western looks" and ability to pronounce and mostly understand Japanese words and names. I was only a college freshman and had agreed with my family to put my education on hold to help pay for my mom's extraordinary medical expenses. Prior to this, I'd worked a few part-time odd jobs in middle school and high school, and that was the extent of my (in)experience.

The firm had very strict and often inexplicable rules. I once called home to check on my mom after she began chemo, and the owner asked me to reimburse him the seventy-five cents for the call, then told me not to ever do that again. Remember, this was way before cell phones.

I was also encouraged to dress in an "extra feminine" way. Huh? It truly felt like falling down the rabbit hole.

One of my personal avatars for my life is Alice in Wonderland. I've often fallen into the surreal. I've felt larger or smaller, and caterpillars have transformed into cats. The world has been filled with bizarre characters like the Red Queen, the White Rabbit, the Cheshire Cat, and the Mad Hatter, with seemingly insoluble riddles, labyrinths, a constant game of truth or dare, and being coerced into participating in the drama or problems of others. Alice herself says early on, "But I don't want to go among mad people." The Cheshire Cat is happy to respond, "You can't help that! We're all mad here."

Throughout it all, Alice remains fearless, inquisitive, firmly rooted in common sense, and self-possessed. No matter what happens to her, Alice remains truly and completely herself. An amazing feat for any of us.

Resume: Ticket to Ride

Just a brief word before we get to the actual interview: your resume matters.

You can fake it 'til you make it, but don't create a fiction novel out of your resume. Do find ways to make your background, including unique skills and experiences, more compelling.

There are thousands of great books written about resumes and people who will help you write yours for a fee. Or you can ask friends, school resources, neighbors, or family who are experienced veterans. (My husband, thanks to his extensive career, recruiting experience and his decades in the C-suite, is an example of a great person to review a resume). Seek quality help in crafting yours. It is your story, and it's often the first impression people get of you. Own it. Don't embellish unnecessarily but embrace the offbeat or unusual. It gives you a chance to be seen from a piece of paper (or pdf!) alone. Focus on the accomplishments within your experience, not just a recitation of job duties. For example, as editor of the school newspaper, I was able to get our school national exposure or I improved the efficiency of the night shift at my after-school job or I did a food drive in my neighborhood during the pandemic. You have done some incredible things and helped people in ways that you didn't think of as leadership but are.

Interviewing: Your Portal to the Future

The general rule for an interview, from the standpoint of the company, is that the applicant should talk about 80 percent of the time, and the employer (whichever person is designated to talk to about this position—and there can be several or just one, depending on the job, the company, and their hiring philosophy) talks for only 20 percent. The mistake that most interviewers (including me sometimes) make is that they talk too much and spend their time selling the applicant on the job rather than trying to genuinely learn about the person in front of them. Will they fit into the culture of the firm? Will they be able to handle the technical requirements of the job? Do they have the right skills?

However, it's ultimately in YOUR best interests to be an active participant in the interview and ask as many questions as you can because you don't win if you get the wrong job. I would define that as one that plays to your weaknesses, not your strengths, or one that doesn't really interest you or has some requirements that you can't or don't want to do (like, come into the office four days a week, drive a long distance, travel a lot, work weekends, work odd hours, and so on). That's just a recipe for failure, which, as we'll discuss, is an opportunity to learn. But it's also an opportunity to feel disappointed and rejected, and we should try to spare ourselves the pain of an own goal, where you accidentally inflict pain on yourself by scoring a goal—for your opponent.

I've had interviews that lasted hours, some that lasted less than fifteen minutes, some in the office, and some over lunch or dinner. It's unlikely that your first interview will be in an unconventional setting (and if it is, one might wonder why). Typically, your interview will be at the office/ place of business. As you become more senior in your career, you may wish to keep discussions about changing firms confidential and would likely meet somewhere more discreet. Therefore, you could be meeting in a restaurant, club, or somewhere off the beaten path.

I was once asked to meet for an "interview" at a place in Los Angeles called the Spearmint Rhino. I gracefully declined that opportunity, as I wasn't sure that my skills were suited for that job. I was once asked to "act out" my "spirit animal" in pantomime. Passed on that one.

You may be interviewing with multiple companies and multiple people, so it's going to test your endurance, versatility, and every single one of your social skills. A sense of humor and excellent manners can buy you a lot of grace. If you have someone who can practice mock interviews with you, I encourage you to do it. It takes a while to adjust to the rhythm of the typical Q&A, and you need to be ready for some curveballs. As part of my time as a career advisory mentor at USC Marshall School of Business, I've done hundreds of mock interviews with my students.

It's not uncommon these days to do an interview via Zoom or another online platform in place of in real life (IRL), so that presents another set of issues. Be sure you're very comfortable with the platform you're using. It's worth it to have your own Zoom account, WebEx, or whichever one most of the prospective employers you're looking at use.

Practice using it with your parents, or roommates, or besties. You still (almost always) have the risk of technical difficulties or glitches, but in this new era of virtual meetings and conversations, excuses are getting to the "dog ate my homework" stage, and they increase the stress, which is undesirable. Back in the old times, we had to worry about traffic and car issues (I've had more than my share of flat tires, dead batteries, dumb accidents, and citations), and we really couldn't recover from being late for an interview.

Today, you may not get to an in-person interview until you're several steps into the process. With virtual interviewing, don't do the pajama bottoms and bunny slippers below the shirt and jacket. You may have to jump up because the dog has choked on a bone, the cat spilled your coffee, your child is having a meltdown, or a police officer or a confused delivery driver is locked in relentless combat with your doorbell. Dress like you would for a "real" interview. In the next chapter, I've included detailed thoughts on what to wear in the workplace, but you need to use the same good judgment and sense of style in the interview. This isn't a virtual happy hour or an update call with your mom.

An interview is your first and ONLY chance to make a first impression; always keep that in mind.

Look Who's Talking: Practical Tips for Your Turn

There are questions you MUST ask (because you really don't know what you don't know). And there's research that you MUST do.

If you have an opportunity to talk to some other women, minorities, or younger people in the company, it might be very helpful. Find out as much as you can about the onboarding, training, orientation, and any windows into corporate culture. People will be guarded—they don't know you, and if there are any odd issues, they won't be ready to share and trust you. This is always the delicate balance in job hunting—trying to find the "right" job for where you are in your life and getting as close to reality as you can from the outside. Time and experience give you additional tools to get more from the interview process, but from the beginning, your powers of observation and instincts are your best friends.

External Sources of Information

There are now some blogs out there that share (mostly) negative stories and comments from those inside companies and industries. But please keep in mind that people who post tend to be upset or frustrated about something, and those who feel like it's all fine remain quiet. As you already know, information that appears on a company website is going to have been carefully curated; it's always going to present all things in the best possible light. We still live in a world where you can't really know what your work experience will be like (unless you have a family member or close friend at the same company), so as much as you possibly can, choose wisely. Again, trust those instincts!

Bring a notebook with you. (It's less disruptive than an iPad and sends a message of competence with humility.) And take LOTS of notes about the salary, salary range, hours you're expected to work, benefits, and expectations.

In addition to the issues above, be sure to ask how many days/hours, if any, you're required to be physically in the office and how many would be remote. One note about remote work: some folks have mentioned that their employers have a camera trained on their computer to almost spy on them. I would find that frightening—very *1984* (George Orwell). Try to learn as much of what you don't know as possible. **I have a current Rock the Interview Checklist available as noted in the beginning of the book.**

While the objective in a search for a job, including the interview process, has historically been viewed as getting an offer, I would suggest that you define it more broadly. To truly be a win for you, you need to do as much as you can to select an opportunity where you feel you can learn, grow, and be excited about. You'll discover much, good and bad, and it will help you better define what's best for you.

Let the games begin!

Chapter 2

"We're the People Who Can Find Whatever You May Need. We Got Everything You Want, Honey, and We Know the Names."

You're now on the metaphorical go space on your personal game board, and you're ready (or not?) to begin the adventure of your life—even if you don't realize YET what you want, what you can accomplish, and what you may have to do or experience. But you WILL.

Life (including your career) isn't about the destination. Yep, that cliché, "It's the journey, not the destination," is very true. Think about any road trips you've taken over the years. Have you gotten off the beaten path to see The World's Largest Thermometer (a personal favorite of mine in Baker, California) or drive on the Enchanted Highway of North Dakota and had a wonderful (or hilariously awful?) outing as a result? Those detours can lengthen the journey, which isn't necessarily bad. Sometimes, where we think we need to go isn't actually where we need to be. Take a moment on that one. And for later in your career, you should remember that what got you to there will keep you from getting to where you want to go next. But I am getting ahead of myself.

You're at the first stop in the jungle. Mind the hippos! I want to share with you a few of the resources you'll need in your environment, as well as some of the unwritten rules of corporate behavior.

Workplace Policies and Practice

Diversity, Equity, Inclusion, and Accessibility (DEI or DEIA)

This is the current hot topic and one of the most measured and discussed metrics for corporations and professional service firms everywhere. It can be very real, or it can be a perfunctory "check the boxes" exercise. If you look at the people who are interviewing you, the leaders of the firm, and who in the organization is ultimately responsible for DEI, it will tell you a lot of what you need to know. Is it a robust and inclusive list of programs for those who need a voice or a safe space? Or is it merely limited to "we train people not to harass or exercise unconscious bias"? Are there ongoing meetings, workshops, and events that support the goal of inclusivity and sharing of issues, ideas, and inspiring speakers? Are there groups you can join if you get the job?

This is important to you because it shows you if DEIA (YOURS, specifically) is truly valued and appreciated or is still more tolerated than celebrated.

In some parts of the United States, companies and governments are arguing to opt out of ANY DEI. This concerns me greatly. I felt that during the sixties, seventies, eighties, and up to recent times, we were making significant progress, and it breaks my heart to see people actively reject progress on all levels. This is happening at a time when there are new pressures: how to best conduct business post-global pandemic (and possibly plan for future outbreaks); deal with seismic legislative changes, like the Dobbs decision reversing *Roe v. Wade*; attract and retain talent; address social isolation; manage a multigenerational workforce; and create a collaborative culture.

This is also a moment when there's a lot of pressure on gender dynamics. Women are 47 percent of the workforce (which decreased during the pandemic as women were torn between their jobs and all the family responsibilities that seem to "naturally" fall to them).[2] But women are gaining slowly on boards. Currently they make up 44.7 percent of Fortune 500 boards and 32.2 percent of C-suite positions. Women are the recipients of 57.7 percent of new bachelor's degrees, 61.4 percent of master's degrees, and 55.2 percent of doctoral degrees. They make up 51 percent of the classes of new doctors and 55.2 percent of new lawyers. However, there remains a disconnect between academic success in undergraduate or graduate education and success at the top for women.

As for younger men, they're also struggling with their career path. They feel anxiety about whether their gender will hold them back and how they should behave in the workplace. For young men, stay strong. Your contribution is necessary and will ensure a better company, community, country, and world. And we need to remember to include EVERYONE and not assume that groups that may have had an advantage historically may or may not now. They may actually be struggling in this present moment.

2. Judith Warner, "Fact Sheet: The Women's Leadership Gap," Center for American Progress, americanprogress.org, March 7, 2014, https://www.americanprogress. org/article/fact-sheet-the-womens-leadership-gap/.

According to some of the most respected social scientists of our time, we're seeing a moment in history when it feels like no one wins. Everyone seems unhappy, frustrated, and unable to find what they're looking for. We struggle to reconcile the rights of the individual with the benefits of a solid social fabric. Life is a team sport, and you can choose your position on the team. You can be the coach, the rock star, the team parent, or the goalie. This is your time to figure out where you best fit.

Vignesh Karthi said, "I'm seeking for someone to help me so that someday, I will be the someone to help some other one."[3]

We're truly in this together. The more we try to deny that and make people we disagree with "other" or "the enemy," the more we're destined to rely on flawed information to make decisions, repeat bad behavior, ignore history, and continue to have a divided world where people feel unsafe and attacked.

Health Insurance

Will this potential employer's medical, dental, life, and disability insurances cover you? If you're full-time, the answer is almost always yes. (You may choose to opt out if you're covered by another plan, for example.) Sometimes, people who work less than a certain number of hours aren't covered. And it's important to make sure that you're being treated fairly. If the potential employer is playing games with hours to avoid giving you the benefits that all workers are entitled to, that's a red

---

3. Vignesh Karthi, according to Goodreads, Goodreads Quotes, accessed October 1, 2023, https://www.goodreads.com/quotes/877352-yes-i-m-seeking-for-someone-to-help-me-so-that.

flag. **I have a checklist that can guide you; please sign up at the beginning of the book.**

There are also social components: Is your partner or spouse covered whether you're in a heteronormative marriage or a domestic partnership? If relevant, see if abortion is covered. Is it still legal in your state? If not, would your employer pay for travel to a state where it is legal? Believe me, I NEVER thought we would be wrestling with these questions in 2024.

I'm merely pointing out some important facts that you need to be aware of and/or questions you may need answers to. Only you know which issues are most important to you, but they can have a tremendous impact on your future.

You may find one day that one of your children or another family member has gender dysphoria and needs more extensive medical care. Insurance coverage for treatment has become a political flashpoint over the past decade, and it's causing great suffering. Regardless of your own personal feelings, there are people, including children, who are on a painful personal journey and are being discriminated against and prevented from seeking any medical attention. We continue to forget that *health care is a human right.*

Not only is health insurance an extremely important issue, but it has historical significance. I had the incredible privilege of being an adviser to President Obama on the Affordable Care Act. It was a key lesson in how democracies can get real things done.

I feel so passionately about equal access to health insurance because my father and I lived a nightmare with my mom's cancer. Insurance hadn't yet caught up with science, and many of the treatments that were needed to keep my mom alive weren't covered at the time. As I shared earlier, I made the decision, along with both of my parents, that I wouldn't go to college full-time. Instead, I would get a job to help with the costs and find a way to put myself through college so that my parents' lifetime savings could go to her cancer treatment. This was one of the greatest challenges of my life. I was eighteen, with a starter job and an acceptance letter from my dream school, the University of Southern California, and I had to talk the bank out of foreclosing on my parents' mortgage on the house that I'd grown up in because my mother had taken care of all the household bills and fallen behind when the cancer spread to her brain. I did ultimately graduate five years after my mom's passing.

My father was working double shifts at Rockwell International, so he only came home to shower, change, check in on my mom and me, sleep a few hours a night, and go back to work. I know firsthand how devastating uncovered medical expenses can be, and I remember what it felt like to know that if we just had a little bit more money, we could keep my mom from dying until we found a solution or even a cure. I took the bus some days to downtown Los Angeles, worked a ten-hour day, went to school three days a week and got home to help make dinner when I could and take the night shift some nights to give my dad a break.

I felt like a failure for not being successful enough to keep my mother alive. My father was a World War II hero (paratrooper in the 101st Airborne) who willingly risked his life at the ripe old age of seventeen (he fudged his age by a few months to be able to sign up to jump out of airplanes and fight) to keep America and democracy safe from tyranny and to honor his parents' dangerous journey to America, which allowed him to grow up free. He also felt like his life was a failure because he didn't know how to save my mom. But the truth is that, with the benefit of hindsight, I can see now that we couldn't have saved her. Technology and medicine were not where they are now, and while money could have possibly prolonged her life, no cure was available at the time at any cost. But that painful experience, with its uncertainty and fear, has made me a committed advocate for better and more inclusive health care for everyone. Many people are one major medical emergency away from losing their savings or risking their home or their future. My situation could have resulted in my never finishing my education, getting sidetracked with stressful debt, and having a very different path. It's something to evaluate carefully and plan for as best as you can.

I hope and believe that both of my parents knew how much I loved them and how their incredible bravery during this time and all their lives gave me strength, courage, and grace. They've significantly defined my life. Mother and Daddy, you're my forever heroes!

Days off for Illness

With more flexible work-from-home options, it's easier to accommodate your (or your child's) illness, so it's even more important to be mindful of taking care of both you and your family while also staying connected to your job. A day when you're working remote allows you to fit in lab appointments, dental appointments, and other routine things with just the time saved from your commute.

Despite a more open environment for discussing mental health issues, you want to be judicious in how you talk about your own. It's private, which is NOT to say it's embarrassing or shameful at all. It just might be wise to be discreet about saying things like, "I need a mental health day," or "I'm just too depressed today," or "I'm in therapy," or "I'm having treatment that day and can't make the meeting." I'm NOT suggesting that you shouldn't be in touch with these feelings or that you shouldn't be seeking help to cope because, right now, we ALL need a little help. And I, as I've shared with you, have struggled with depression almost as long as I can remember. I allowed that to lead me into several unfortunate situations and to make some very questionable decisions. I see a therapist, I believe in alternative therapy, and I believe in doing the work and actively moving toward a better understanding of myself and how I can be better and do better.

So what should you do, or how should you handle the situation? If you have medical appointments during business hours (which is, of course, fine), you may share the purpose or not. It's your decision. I prefer as much privacy as I can get because it feels like there's way less of it now. But providing some information about your absence and timing is basic courtesy. Try to avoid being gone during peak periods of work if possible.

Many things have an impact on your mental well-being. You do want to be sure that the firm or company offers programs for help when you need it or at least has some flexibility for you to craft your own mental health program by making time for exercise, therapy, or treatment without requiring shaming or unnecessary approvals. You can get a basic idea of what the benefits are in your interview. And when you join an organization, you get onboarded and get a packet of information. Also, try to ask any specific questions then if you can.

Parental Leave

For most people, becoming parents through birth or adoption is not only one of the major milestones of their lives but one of the first introductions to our health care system for a significant event. What's covered and what's not, as well as how much leave is given, is so important to a new or prospective parent.

Fortunately, like so many things, the world has changed for the better. Things were still pretty grim when I decided to have children. It was later in my career, and one of the consequences was that it made my pregnancy riskier and more complicated.

At eight months, I began bleeding and was ordered on bed rest. I had to beg for time off so I didn't lose my baby (my son, now twenty-seven). I had to agree to take calls from bed 24/7 and take a pay cut. It was a VERY different time. In fact, I waited four months before I told anyone I was pregnant (I'd experienced two miscarriages, so it was partly out of caution) because I didn't want anyone to think I wasn't going to be serious about my career after becoming a mom. During those four months, I got lots of unflattering comments about my weight.

Once I told him, my boss was NOT supportive. This was the man who was past his prime, to put it tactfully, and took credit for ALL my work to justify his exorbitant salary and expense account, while I, on the verge of starting a family and not totally comfortable that we could afford everything that entailed, had to continue doing my work (and his!) at great risk to my health. I was also told that being given any leave was a major favor, which I would need to repay.

When I returned to work, the pressure was beyond enormous. The system was flawed and broken. I had a C-section with major complications and barely got five weeks of paid leave, and I had to beg for another week of unpaid leave. My memories of that time are clouded a bit by grief that both my parents were gone, and I felt their absence profoundly from my son's (and my) life. It would have been so magical, but it wasn't to be. Acknowledging and dealing with the losses and blows life presents, even during the best of times, is key to moving forward.

It's better for new moms and dads now. I share this story to provide some history and some hope that things will (and must) continue to improve. If we truly value children and parenting in our society, we need to craft policies that support that. This is a big part of what I fought for, and I hope that my struggles were part of the price of a better future for the next generations. There's always a price; nothing is ever free. Someone has to pay it, and sometimes that's you.

Flexible Hours or Hybrid Work Practices

It's too soon yet to say for sure, but the final answer seems clear to me. (We'll see how it plays out in our sort of post-COVID world.) But the days of going into an office five days a week and working long days sitting at a desk or in a cubicle aren't a popular idea any longer with many employees. There are some powerful leaders who say this is a bad long-term strategy for American business, including Jamie Dimon of JP Morgan, Arvind Krishna of IBM, and David Risher of Lyft, to name just a few.[4] Still, it's hard to argue against the benefits of having at least some working hours be remote.

---

4. Marguerite Ward, "Some CEOS are pushing workers to return to the office, but it could come with a cost: Hurting diversity," Business Insider, January 28, 2023, https://www.businessinsider.com/remote-work-return-to-office-wfh-diversity-jamie-dimon-2023-1.

I've found that when working remote, I'm able to do the strategic and creative thinking I struggle to find time for when I have a daily commute and a constant stream of interruptions in the office. I've been able to positively correlate my extra time for thinking and planning with financial benefits for my firm, as well as for others, when I can structure my time differently. I'm more willing to travel to meet with people and spend true quality time with them. I've had conversations with clients, colleagues, and industry and world leaders that I couldn't have imagined in the past.

But at the same time, I really miss the people. Our industry, insurance and financial services, like so many, is an apprenticeship business. If you aren't together with your team and your leader, working on projects in real life, you lose precious learning opportunities and the tangible benefits of active real-time collaboration. It's easy to have communication challenges when you aren't talking to each other live. And if you have clients, you MUST see them. Otherwise, you may have seven days off every week because there will be no clients.

I believe we'll settle on a compromise—a hybrid solution. This allows flexibility so people can have more balanced lives (and we do all benefit from that and become better human beings capable of doing more creative things when this is true) while at the same time keeping people connected to each other, creating opportunities to bond, learn from each other, and grow.

This will also have the effect of making the time spent in the office more valuable, more efficient, and more meaningful. Despite its overuse, the term *quality time* is a real thing for the times we're living in.

As artificial intelligence (AI) becomes more real (but with an unknown impact), some view it as an existential threat. It's more important than ever to focus on what humans are hardwired for in their DNA: connection and purpose. We've survived and thrived over millennia through our social connections and sense of community. We need the company of other humans.

Multiple studies during the pandemic showed that we now have a global epidemic of loneliness. It is as deadly as smoking a dozen cigarettes a day and costs the health care industry billions of dollars a year. The number of people living alone has surged to a record 29 percent, nearly a third of the US population. Prior to 2019, three in five people reported being lonely, but post-pandemic, this already alarming number has increased, particularly among young people. Surgeon General Vivek Murphy declared in 2023 that loneliness is officially an epidemic.[5]

Lack of social interaction and support from our peers literally harms our physical and mental health. We see the fraying of family and community bonds, a lack of purpose, and pressure from external forces among all age groups, including seniors.

What Do I Wear? Every Woman's Existential Crisis, Now Available to Men Too

Fortunately, things have changed since I entered the workforce. I do remember being fairly traumatized when one of my female managers (in the eighties) told me that the way I dressed wasn't "serious" enough

---

5. "New Surgeon General Advisory raises alarm about the devastating impact of the epidemic of loneliness and isolation in the United States," Office of the Assistant Secretary for Health (OASH), HHS.gov, May 3, 2023, https://www.hhs.gov/about/news/2023/05/03/new-surgeon-general-advisory-raises-alarm-about-devastating-impact-epidemic-loneliness-isolation-united-states.html.

and screamed "high school attire." Then she happily presented me with *The Woman's Dress for Success Book* by John Molloy, written in 1977 (His first *Dress for Success Book* for men was published in 1975.) Yep. 1977.

It was a very different time, but some of the core themes still hold.

Dress like you already have the job when you interview, dress like you belong when you get there, and dress to project confidence and competence, always. If you aren't in the fashion industry, don't go crazy. If you're in a service business where you ask potential clients for large sums of money, your appearance is a factor in their decision to choose you . . . or not. If you look sloppy, disorganized, or just plain bad, they may feel that you're not responsible or not someone they can trust with their business, their money, and their future. I've learned that having people trust you with their money —in whatever form, whether investment, risk mitigation, resources, or time—is one of the most powerful compliments you can ever receive. It's also one of the hardest things to achieve.

My early experiences came at the beginning of the concept of power dressing. Malloy's book was an immediate bestseller on the *New York Times* Best Seller list, has sold millions and millions of copies, and inspired clothing drives, conversations, rebellion, awareness, and conversation. And it still has solid principles to teach us.

As recently as 2019, studies by image consultants showed that women with chipped nails or messy hair were deemed "unqualified" by male colleagues or bosses. And if you overdo your makeup or use too much perfume or lotion (or the "wrong" fragrance), you further erode your credibility. It does feel at times that you only get opportunities to be judged, shamed, and dismissed, but never rewarded. Doing a dizzying number of small things or making even the simplest choice quickly becomes a quagmire of self-doubt, anxiety, and confusion. The price of admission is perfection, and the price of a minor infraction is to justify the disrespect that you're probably being treated with anyway. Oh, and you have to be attractive, but not TOO attractive.

I, however, was horrified at the time. Not only did I not own anything suitable, but I was only making $800 a month back then. I moved back in with my parents (my mom, as you now know, was ill, and we'd just learned she was already in advanced stage 3 of the cancer that took her from us too soon), and I looked awful in bow ties. Yes, you read that right. Bow ties for women on white button-up blouses that were truly unflattering. And shoulder pads! I still shudder involuntarily when I see them to this day. I thought then that Brooks Brothers was a restaurant! I simply had no idea. When I went into the store, I couldn't afford anything there. It was disheartening, to say the least.

My mom, forever the Southern belle she was, had a simple instruction for me: "Don't go out looking like a hoochie mama." For those of you unaccustomed to Southern slang, a hoochie mama generally gets paid for her services, but they aren't the traditional corporate tasks. I jokingly used this reference once with a female partner of mine, and she looked at me aghast, then said, "I don't have anything in my wardrobe that can possibly be viewed as 'hoochie mama' clothing!"

Hmm . . . I definitely have a few! Well, there's always one, right?

But what my mother did teach me is that you can dress well on a budget. She always did, and she had a highly visible mid-level management job dealing with the public at a store called Fedco. It's no longer in existence, but it was a retail force back in the day. I recommend going to discount stores, such as T.J. Maxx, Marshalls, and others. Or try eBay to buy high-quality clothing at the lowest price possible.

Because of my earlier experiences with the wardrobe police, I held on too long to a rigid dress style. Finally, I was given the opportunity to work with MAC Cosmetics in Canada prior to their acquisition by Estée Lauder. Their team was mostly young women who were much bolder and cooler than I, working in fashion for a red-hot new cosmetics company. They told me straight out that I was "too young to dress so old." They made me sit down with one of their cosmetic consultants to "shake up" my look. My hair . . . Well, best left unsaid.

And the wonderful, effortlessly chic women of MAC told me that I was "frumpy" and "dated." It's important to know when to just lean in and listen! It was awkward, but I was very grateful to get the employee discount on all my new products to update my new, more "hip" look.

In my sixties, I finally feel empowered to follow my own style comfortably. It's taken years of treading the fine line between candor and cruelty, not to mention CONSTANT judgment by both men and women.

Men have a uniform from day one, and as much as they complain on the odd occasion today when they must wear a tie or dress jacket, they know what's "correct" and what's not. Yet I still see young men dressing like they're going to their high school football game. Please don't. There is a benefit to knowing the uniform!

Women have so many choices but so little guidance. There are still many opportunities to make some unfortunate choices that can hurt their image and reputation. The fashion industry seems to be occasionally at war with women.

For everyone: learn what works for you and what's "required" to look appropriate for your firm, your clients, or your customers, and mix it up with your own fashion sense or a little flair. We sublimate the messages in our brain that we can interpret as bragging or showboating, but you know what works for you and what doesn't when it comes to clothes. Go shopping with anyone who identifies as a woman for a bathing suit and take along a lot of Xanax.

We know what colors, what type of neckline, and what cut of jacket, dress, slacks, or hybrid outfit works best for us. As I mentioned, you don't have to spend a lot of money to look like a literal million bucks. Later, when you have a lot of money, you can still be mindful of ways to save money, save the environment (sustainability), and create an even more custom and unique look, since you'll have many more options.

The best approach applies to everyone: dress to inspire confidence in you and your audience.

I've followed the lead of younger women I work with, and it's been quite freeing to be able to wear pretty much what I really like while being mindful of a few guidelines (as opposed to an entire book dictating every decision, including frequency of dry cleaning—another wardrobe expense that can be shocking). Someone recently described me as "a fashionista," and while I was very flattered, I burst into laughter. I call it a victory if both my shoes match most days and I brushed my hair AND my teeth, but I do try. Lord knows, I try.

Make Friends with IT

As with all things, those who own and control the technology seem to rule us all and have great control and influence over our day-today lives (and this also makes the issue of AI more critical to observe and evaluate). I've known and worked with many IT professionals throughout my career and personal life. They're extremely skilled, but they're still human beings. If you want to move to the top of their list when you have a glitch (and you will, often) or don't know how to do something, you need to remember that they're your colleagues, not servants. I thank them for their help always, sometimes bring them treats, and whenever possible, support their promotions and recognitions. I was recently thrilled to support the promotion of our primary IT person to senior vice president; he's been an enormous help to me since day one of my current firm (twenty-three years), and he wanted to make a change recently to content creation for our internal and external communications.

Be a mensch if you want to connect to your email in the middle of Africa at 2:00 a.m. (yep, that's been me!). Having a good relationship with IT can help you make sure you have someone to call when the lions are outside your tent, you need to work but can't connect to the internet or the network and said lions are unimpressed with your technology or your issues. But they will be visualizing you as dinner!

Emails

We could write an entire book on this topic and its endless subpoints, but I'll try to keep it brief since so many have already written excellent books and guidelines.

Emails live forever and ever. You need to be very careful about what you say and how you say it. Mind your manners, check your spelling and punctuation, and try to be brief but informative, and think long and hard before you say something regrettable. Also, please be SUPER careful about hitting "Reply All"; don't do it if you have any hesitation. Either respond just to the one person you intend to or make sure that your boss isn't copied on an email where you are trashing them! "Reply All" should be used sparingly.

Abuse doesn't have to be aloud or in person; bad behavior can be communicated very effectively through email or text. In fact, as we see across all social media, it's much easier to speak out from behind a screen. And this is leading to normalization of boundary crossing, saying things that are just not okay, or violating etiquette rules (all caps IS shouting, and I don't like to be shouted at). Try to think how you would feel after receiving the email you're composing. You don't have to strive for daily inspirational bon mots, but try not to be too brief, blunt, or passive-aggressive.

Human Resources

While it may seem counterintuitive, Human Resources (HR) isn't necessarily your advocate. Their first responsibility is to the firm, and if they don't make that their priority, they're not doing their job.

HR people are often your first port of entry when you're hired. Their role, after you're hired, is to get you properly onboarded and set up properly. It can be easy and wise to cultivate relationships with them. They tend to be engaging, knowledgeable, and helpful people. You should just exercise some caution in knowing that nothing you say to them is truly confidential, and it's not a good place to vent your frustrations. Although, if you're experiencing serious issues like bullying, harassment, etc., you should make a formal complaint or have a conversation that can help you find a solution. They can also be great advocates and problem solvers, and they have great institutional knowledge. Use your relationships here wisely.

Administrators and Assistants

People's executive assistants are powerful gatekeepers. They're always protective of their principal and guard their calendars, phones, and office (and thus their time and energy). My EA is someone I refer to as "The Sister of My Heart," and we're close. It's always a good idea to befriend key EAs because if they like you, they can facilitate entry to the precious time of the person you want or need to see. And I don't mean that as a solely manipulative tactic.

There's a line in *Pretty Woman* when the girlfriend du jour of Richard Gere's character informs him that she's breaking up with him. He's truly shocked—even more so when she says, "I spend more time talking to your assistant than to you." Then he runs into another former flame at a party and asks her if she felt the same way. He is having trouble believing that either of these women have a real relationship with the assistant, but his former flame informs him, "I just got married; I was tired of waiting for you. She was one of my bridesmaids."

I think this is a wonderful example of how reaching out in support of your goals can also lead to a lovely friendship or relationship that you might not have ever had. We all respond to courtesy, respect, and positive attention. You can never go wrong, as my mama used to say, by "being the kind of person you'd like to be around. You can always use another friend, and there's always room for one more at the table if there's room in your heart."

Investment

You don't have to be Warren Buffett, Mark Zuckerberg, or a newly minted billionaire to make good investments, whether it be of time or treasure. You can invest small or slowly, and you can do it in things that support your passion (socially conscious investments), engage you in the stock market, or deepen your understanding of our economy. A mentor or a very knowledgeable friend can be a blessing here (I married a chief financial officer, but there are many ways!). Do reach out to others for guidance and help.

Retirement Plan/Savings

Yep, I'm going to be your mom for a moment. Even if you're twenty-two and immortal, you must start saving for your future. I wouldn't even think of it as "retirement planning"; I suggest calling it a Freedom Fund. At each decade of your life from now until retirement or whatever personal milestones you've set for yourself, this will become increasingly important to your quality of life. Your generation has a chance to redefine longevity of life, but you'll want to be certain that you have considered and planned for your financial longevity as well.

I see people my age who are one paycheck away from disaster at a time when they should be living their best existence and enjoying the benefits of having spent many years working hard. It is never too late to make your life better and your future more secure. But as we get older, and depending on our health, our options become more limited. That's why you would ideally start when you're young. If it's a deduction from your weekly check for a 401(k), an IRA, or an online stock trading account, it's all good. You can give up certain things. (That $8 latte at Starbucks can be reserved for treat days or special celebrations because a share of Starbucks stock—trading at $97 today, up from $82 a year ago—is waaay better for you than a year of daily lattes, chai tea, or Frappuccinos. Honest!)

Bottom line, if your employer matches up to a certain percentage contribution from you, give that amount. If you don't, you're refusing to take extra money that your company wants to give you.

When I first started working, the ERISA laws weren't as robust as they are now, so I couldn't even qualify to put money away until I was twenty-five. I wasted seven years of working and not being able to put money away. And I didn't initially put in the full amount. But a friend sat me down and did a very basic chart, practically with crayons, and I saw the error of my ways.

Conclusion

You've now gotten settled in your base camp. You know who has access to information or people you may need. You're getting the hang of the "right" wardrobe. You're thinking about your financial future and sort of understand your health insurance and what's expected in terms of practices and policies. And you know how DEIA impacts or benefits you. It's time to take the next steps and watch out for the hazards around you!

Chapter 3

"You Can Taste the Bright Lights, But You Won't Get Them for Free"

"I shot through my twenties like a luminous thread through a dark needle; blazing toward my destination, Nowhere."[6]

I'm with Carrie on this one. (RIP to a shining star.) And I'm here to help you be better prepared, more focused, happier, and . . . alive. We need to always continue to believe in ourselves, our value, our endurance, and the power of our dreams.

Issues of Morality: Laws of the Jungle or Civilization?

Don't lose your moral compass. On our safari, we'll have a few compasses to refer to, but this one's a biggie.

A client and dear friend of mine recently paid me the incredible compliment of saying that I have "an unmatched moral compass." History has shown us the folly and fallacy of "just following orders" and that you'll ultimately pay a price, either from self-inflicted pain

---

6. Carrie Fisher, *Postcards from the Edge* (New York: Pocket Books, 2002).

or social or legal consequences. Do the right things because you can. Because that's what you want to do and what you believe in.

It's sometimes very hard (usually, in fact!) to always do the right thing. But what distinguishes leaders from followers is the ability to make the RIGHT judgment call and do the RIGHT thing, especially when it's hard and you don't really want to, frankly. Be clear on your own compass. It takes time to shape your beliefs, and as life goes on, you'll likely see many more shades of gray than black and white.

You'll never go wrong doing the right thing, especially when no one is looking. As you progress in your career, there will be harder choices, obstacles, and situations. Determining the right thing in and of itself isn't easy either. Stay the course, always.

One of my favorite high school teachers said something that resonated with me and still does. He said, "Be the kind of person that dogs, cats, and babies like." His point was that babies and animals have a kind of sixth sense about people, as they're not influenced by external factors. They judge based on what they see in front of them and what their primal instincts tell them. This advice has always been firmly lodged in my mind.

The Power of Others

I invite you to reflect on the power of the people in your life who have changed it for the better, whether they be family, friends, colleagues, bosses, or even adversaries.

Over the course of my life, I've had some incredible mentors, advisers, and leaders who I've learned from; there were also people who were an object lesson in what NOT to do. But by far, the amazing people outweighed the less amazing ones, and many of them have absolutely and affirmatively changed my life. Those people are out there for you too. Being open to possibilities and meeting lots of different people helps move that process along.

I also mention adversaries. We often learn a great deal about ourselves from the people who challenge us in an uncomfortable way. Often, these people aren't intending us any goodwill, but we can convert their intended ill will into a life lesson and an opportunity to see ourselves from a different perspective. This may include some weaknesses or negative aspects of us; that knowledge gives you the power to change and get stronger.

I recently watched an interview with Tyler Perry, in which he said, "Some people come into our lives for a season, not for forever, but there is always a reason."[7] That has been my experience with the great, good, and bad people in my life. Embrace the lessons.

Knowledge

It's the one thing no one can ever take away from you. Learn, learn, learn. If you're fortunate enough to find a job in an industry that resonates with your passions, that's an easier task than if you don't. But regardless, find a way to dig in and learn more. When we're young, it's easy to take for granted that our brains work faster, retain information, and process it quickly. At the same time, we don't yet have a wealth of experiences that give us a deeper understanding of ourselves and

---

7. A1 Inspiration, "SOME PEOPLE ARE ONLY FOR A SEASON IN YOU'RE LIFE -- Tyler Perry," YouTube, posted January 2, 2023, https://www.youtube.com/watch?v=vpIA6F7vRyc.

others, so all that fast processing can sometimes lead to impulsive behavior or coming to the wrong conclusions. It's okay. Give yourself some grace. As bright as you are, you'll get brighter still.

In my fifth-grade algebra class, Mr. Weinstock put up a sign for us to see every day that said: "It's What You Learn After You Know It All That Counts." So, so true! And I'm sharing this to encourage you, not to suggest that you don't have the right skills now. Just know that it will get better and easier. I learn something new every day, even when I REALLY do NOT want to. Especially then, even. Life can be an endless series of adventures, learning, or wisdom. Or not. The choice is always yours, and you get to make it anew each day.

To repeat, "It's what you learn after you know it all that counts." That's a constant, and it will be true for your entire life. As you learn those new things, some of them will challenge some of your long-held beliefs. They may force you to revisit those or see if there's another meaning that complements rather than rebukes said belief. And sometimes, you realize that you just didn't know what you didn't know. That happens to me a lot. And I feel blessed to be living now, in a time when so much is available online. I once sent a thank-you note to Sergey Brin and Larry Page for inventing Google just for me! They did write back—a lovely note. Keep learning.

Understanding Your Own Motives

My purpose, I believe, is to be a storyteller. My hope (or dream, if you will) is that by sharing my stories and the resulting lessons and knowledge, I can help others survive, prosper, create their best lives, and lead the way for others.

This understanding can be one of the hardest things to gain. It's one component of your overall life plan. Your motives will change as you yourself change and grow. But we're back to the fundamental question of "What's my why?"

When I was younger, I just wanted everyone to like me. I associated being liked and approved of with happiness, and I believed these were the keys to it. That was partly my nature and partly my belief that some of the roads to getting ahead were closed to me unless someone liked and believed in me enough to grant access. That was true to some extent. However, other people's approval does NOT provide happiness over the long run. In fact, it's quite the opposite.

To this day, I'm often disrespected, which only gives me further purpose and motivation, honestly. I don't need anyone's approval as much these days, but I'd be lying if I said it didn't matter to me. It does. I think it's in our DNA. We need acceptance and approval. But you must run your own race and find your own purpose, accomplishments, and joy.

Other people won't necessarily feel your loss or disappointment or be by your side during a serious health issue, family crisis, or sleepless night when you're wide awake from anxiety, fear, or pain. It's important to develop collaborative relationships and strong friendships and to help others whenever you can. But you do indeed need to put on your own oxygen mask first, just like the airline safety announcements tell you. You must live in your own purpose and find your own happiness, or you can't help anyone else or find your ideal life.

Where Are You on the Work/Life Balance Continuum?

We're programmed to find balance in our lives, which is often elusive. I've found that at any moment, I'm giving 110 percent to one area of my life while another area is going to implode if I don't give it 5 percent I don't have today. The more things you're trying to achieve, the less chance you'll have of making it balance nicely at the end of a day.

One of my current business partners has a saying: "The bumps are harder when you're going a hundred and ten miles per hour vs. thirty toward your future." Only you get to determine what makes you happy and what matters to you. At the end of each day, I take a moment to see if I did my best. Did I focus on the right things today? If not, I have tomorrow (hopefully!), and I will get better at prioritizing and focusing. It's okay. It really is. Just accept that nothing is ever perfectly balanced, your day can get rearranged with five minutes' notice, and you still have ultimate control of your actions and choices. Practice mindfulness and acceptance in addition to those mad planning and organizing skills.

Invest Time and Energy in Your Health and Fitness

Being alive counts for a lot. Trust me. As someone who has had health challenges, made some risky choices, and been in some dangerous situations, alive is awesome. You can't get a single thing done if you're dead. It doesn't matter how you look, what people think of you, or what you're wearing. When you're dead, nothing matters. And all the great things you were going to accomplish never happen. Game over.

This investment is important to develop early in your career to help you deal with stress and feel better in general. It's also worth considering in the middle of your journey and as you look ahead to the rest of your life. To the extent that you can live your life and put less emphasis on what others think and more on what YOU think, you'll be happier, which generally leads to healthier. One of my biggest regrets is that I spent too much time and energy worrying about the opinions of others.

The middle of the journey is also a time when you've been given or taken on many more responsibilities. This creates a scarcity of time to do anything for yourself, so it's hard to stay fit and healthy. But do whatever you can. I try to walk a certain number of miles every day, even the days when I'm working remotely, so I can multitask business and stay alive. You can too!

With stress and the ever-increasing demands on your time as you progress in your career and take on additional personal responsibilities, like starting a family, the more important it is to still take care of yourself. Find something easy you can do anywhere and fit it in whenever or however you can.

Yes, you're young. And you should have fun and enjoy dessert. But it's a good time to cultivate a fitness-and-health mindset so you can be the one partying all night at eighty.

Career, Relationships, and Children

Can you have it all? Maybe? Probably?

Actually, the answer is YES. BUT . . . But not all at the same time or most of the time at the same time. Or perhaps the title of a recent Oscar-winning movie, *Everything Everywhere All at Once*, suggests a strategy?

Nope. It's a constant struggle over priorities. You second-guess yourself every minute of every day. You're often bone weary. Sleep is one of the first casualties of an ambitious journey, a fuller existence, or a steep climb.

You want and should want to have a full and happy life beyond work, even if you're in your dream job.

This relates back to the question of balance. You definitely can have it all, but you can't do . . . well, everything everywhere all at once.

You can have a romantic relationship(s), friendships, and partnerships. Do look for joy, love, and fun. Happiness, like success, isn't a destination; it's a thousand small moments, and a hundred major ones. It's a sunset, a walk with your dog, the sound of the ocean, accomplishing a deeply personal goal, playing chase with your cat, a warm fire, the touch of a loved one's hand, or your child's smile.

If you choose to become a parent, your life will become both more complicated and more joyful. There are times when the demands of your job will come into conflict with your parenting responsibilities, guaranteed. The best solution for this is for BOTH parents to be involved and recognize that they're a team. Put "Divide and Conquer" on the daily to-do list!

You'll learn the art of delicately saying no and learning how to be in two places at once (or at least make it appear so; I can guide you on how to do that!). Be ruthlessly pragmatic about what you should do and where you should be for the overall benefit of you and your family. This constant push/pull isn't for the faint of heart. In all the years when my son was growing up, I had to miss only one event. You can make it work if you're willing to drive, fly, or swim between two or three places (and it's possible unless you have a situation like mine—I was in

London, and it was physically impossible), not worry about sleep too much for a while, and put a little less time into your personal hobbies or interests. It's worth reminding all of us that we do only get one life. But when we choose to have children, we owe them a great start to their life. It's encouraging that more and more fathers are actively involved. My husband and I did divide and conquer for many events, we had great childcare, and we had close friends who helped us enormously. It really does take a village.

Watch for the Hyenas

Hyenas are historically featured in folklore as frightening, cruel, and even evil creatures. Although they're a vital part of the African ecosystem, one could argue that they're also present in the corporate jungle in human form. It's those hyenas walking around on two legs that we're focused on.

It never occurred to me that I didn't need to win the approval of nor did I owe anything to the people who treated me badly (those metaphorical hyenas). I still felt it was my responsibility to fix everything. While many things can be fixed, and I prefer continuity and calm in long-term relationships, sometimes that simply can't be, and I'm willing to let a few of those relationships go now that I'm looking at my life differently. But those of you who still have miles to go, please don't limit yourself.

I remember one person saying to me about thirty years ago that she didn't have room or time for more friends in her life. Given that she was around my age at the time and not even forty, I found this just sad. Yes, there are hyenas out there, but there are also elephants who are calm, strong, and loyal; chimpanzees and monkeys who love to have a good time and entertain; colorful, gentle zebras; lions who assume they're the rock stars; and capybaras (feel free to google), who are considered the friendliest animal on the planet.

So many people must truly believe that they're the Fountain of All Wisdom and Knowledge (not referring to YouTube, TikTok, or social media stars where we have the option to choose—or not—their content). They often spout off their beliefs and values in a judgmental way that suggests that if you would just listen to them or be like them, you, too, would be right and perfect. They're rarely right—especially for YOU. Don't let them get in your head; you already know or will learn how to live YOUR best life. It isn't worth it to live someone else's version of what's best for you. They'll never care or pay the price for all the things that go wrong or make you unhappy. Don't give anyone the keys to your heart, brain, soul, or life. Share your life with the right people, but chart your own course on your own journey.

Please hear this: I would never presume to determine for another human being what's best for them or what makes them happy. Other people seem eager to give me unwelcome feedback or attempt to dictate my choices. We owe each other tolerance, forgiveness, and grace. But you MUST never succumb to the pressure. You're the best judge of what makes YOU happy and successful. And if you follow the advice of others against your own inner voice and are unhappy or fail, they won't be there for you. But they will still judge you for following their advice and not being true to yourself.

It's a dizzying combination of people and choices, but continue to trust your instincts and move forward. There is NOT a "one size fits all" model for living one's life. And if there were, how awful would that be?

Embracing and Coping with Failure

You DO learn more from your failures than your successes. The hard part is getting back up and dusting yourself off. One of my current business partners has a rule he shared that I've tailored for me: give yourself a day to grieve the failure or mistake, then move on and keep moving. I now embrace that, although if it's a big failure, miss, or loss, I give myself a weekend or at least two days. But the point is, get back up and live to fight another day.

I watch and follow many of the great philosophers of our time. The other day, Steven Bartlett, on *The Diary of A CEO*, said he has interviewed thousands of people to ask them if they would choose to undo their moments of greatest failure or pain, and they all said no because they wouldn't be who they are now.[8]

John C. Maxwell is an American speaker, pastor, and author of many books focusing on leadership. In 2014, he was named the number-one leadership and management expert in the world by *Inc. Magazine*, and his books have sold over twenty million copies.

The book of his that most impacted me is *Failing Forward: Turning Mistakes into Stepping Stones for Success*, written in 2000. I was about to leave a job of twenty-three years for many complicated reasons, and I was utterly terrified about the new venture I was embarking upon. I read this book every night for months to gain insight and, yes, courage to take a major risk and fail. If you'll indulge me, I'd like to share a few of the lines that gave me the strength to challenge myself.

---

8. Steven Bartlett, "Steven Bartlett: 'Invest your time wisely' — the entrepreneur shares lessons for leadership success," Think with Google, October 2022, https://www.thinkwithgoogle.com/intl/en-gb/future-of-marketing/management-and-culture/steven-bartlett-lessons-success/.

"If the possibility of failure was erased, what would you attempt to achieve? Failure is simply the price we pay to achieve success. When achievers fail, they view it as a momentary event, not a lifelong epidemic. To conquer fear, you have to feel the fear and take action anyway. That is, after all, the very definition of courage. Life is playing a poor hand well. If we look long enough for what we want in life, we are almost sure to find it. The greatest battle you wage against failure occurs on the inside, not the outside. Success is the journey. Fail forward and fail often."[9]

It's never going to feel good, not ever. But if you're always brutally honest with yourself, you'll gain wisdom and eventually joy from the pain. Truly, "No pain, no gain." And no shortcuts. I wish there were; I would definitely take them! You're strapped in and on the ride. The only way out is through, even if you're going upside down and the tunnel is dark.

And with proper attribution to the amazing Yoda of *Star Wars*, "There is no try. Do or do not."[10]

This may seem like odd advice at the start of your journey. But taking risks to move yourself and your career forward is much easier when you're in your twenties or even thirties than it is at forty. I do know this from personal and sometimes painful experiences. And I've also made major changes at forty, fifty, and sixty. You don't stop evolving and learning if you allow yourself to keep evolving. I played it too safe in the beginning (in a culture that expected women to be quiet and be "a

9. John C. Maxwell, *Failing Forward* (Tennessee: HarperCollins Leadership, 2007).

10. Dan Zehr, *"Empire at 40:* Teaching with *Star Wars*: The Wisdom of 'Do. Or Do Not.'"* StarWars.com, May 13, 2020, https://www.starwars.com/news/empire-at-40-teaching-with-star-wars-the-wisdom-of-do-or-do-not.

good girl"), and I became bolder as I got older. Whatever path unfolds in front of you, stay the course. Trust your instincts. Give 110 percent. (No "lazy girl" or "lazy boy" jobs or "quiet quitting." Make sure that when you do quit, they notice.)

I'm accustomed to being underestimated. It both stings and inspires me to channel my anger into something constructive that will prove everyone wrong and, most importantly, quiet the voices in my head. Believe me, no one can channel my own insecurities and fears better than I can. Whatever you may think about my talent and impact—or rather, my lack thereof—I've already thought it, felt it, lived it.

We're now frequently hearing the term "impostor syndrome." It's life. We all feel (except for narcissists, but their time will come!) that we aren't the real deal, that we don't have any special gifts or qualities that justify whatever it is we're doing. I think it's a sign of real greatness if you're questioning if you're good enough.

I fear disappointment and failure. Both cause deep pain. I believe that all of us have this fear, but some are able to be a bit braver. After all, courage is acting even when you're scared, right? To find that bravery, I've had to understand why I've been so afraid to fail. Part of that fear is my upbringing. My parents, who were amazing and brave human beings, still had a great fear of life's hard blows and told me to always prepare for the worst. I think it was their way of trying to protect me from disappointment, but no one can ever protect us from that. Part of it is my sense of always being "other." I've never really fit in anywhere, and people love to put me in boxes. I've allowed myself to be a prisoner of other people's expectations (and sometimes I truly had no choice, given moments in history). I think younger generations are more comfortable with being "other" than I ever was, but many of them are still truly in pain.

There's a sign I keep in my office that quotes Jack Canfield: "Everything You Want Is on the Other Side of Fear." A dear friend of mine gave me another sign that says: "If You Are Going Through Hell, Act Like You Own the Place!"[11] (Apologies to Winston Churchill for taking his famous quote a little further!)

"Everything you want is on the other side of fear." – Jack Canfield

One of the most powerful examples of an epic fail resulting in overall success is when Coca-Cola decided to switch the original, much-loved formula for their iconic soda (born in Atlanta and considered breakfast of champions by some of my family and sometimes by me!) to New Coke, which extensive taste tests indicated was more popular and tasted better. It was sweeter, similar to Pepsi. BUT the loyal Coca-Cola consumers felt betrayed. Americans have some specific buttons. (If you doubt me, I refer you to the presidential elections of 2016, 2020, and soon, 2024.) And if they feel taken for granted or disrespected by a global brand they've supported for years, there will be consequences.

Sergio Zyman was the senior Coca-Cola marketing representative in the eighties. He actually had two stints at Coca-Cola: from 1979 to 1987 and from 1993 to 1998. He was responsible for the spectacular success of Diet Coke, so he felt confident in his recommendation to switch to New Coke. In the short term, this was a disaster that lost close to half a billion in today's dollars for the company, and Mr. Zyman

---

11. Winston Churchill according to BrainyQuote, "If you're going through hell, keep . . ." BrainyQuote, accessed September 27, 2023, https://www.brainyquote.com/quotes/winston_churchill_103788.

lost his job. He said none of this was a failure—that it was actually a stunning success. His goal all along had been to reclaim the relationship between Coke and consumers. Think about that for a moment. He was addressing a core ingredient/value for the overall success of the company and the brand—the relationship between the buyer and the seller of a beloved product.

When Coke later rebranded and launched the original formula Coca-Cola Classic while keeping New Coke (I mean, they DID pass ALL the taste tests!), it was such an incredible success that Zyman got his job back, and Coke made even more money!

At the end of his reign (he was also referred to as the Aya-Cola, as discussed in Marcia Layton Turner's book *How to Think Like the World's Greatest Marketing Minds*, which is a fantastic read), The Coca-Cola Company was selling more than a billion servings of its products daily and growing at an average of 7 percent a year.[12] As arrogant and provocative as Zyman was reputed to be, he clearly had the right approach to marketing. In his book *The End of Marketing as We Know It*," Zyman states that "Marketing is an act of magic that people have undertaken to protect."[13]

The CEO of Coca-Cola at the time, Donald Keough, said, "Some cynics say we planned the whole thing" as a marketing stunt to expand overall sales. Keough's reply? "We are not that dumb, and we are not

---

12. Matt Kempner, "Keough an affable but tough Coke leader," *Atlanta Journal-Constitution*, ajc.com, February 24, 2015, https://www.ajc.com/business/keough-affable-but-tough-coke-leader/3mJH6FkDAXijjEscdeEQMK/.

13. Sergio Zyman, *The End of Marketing as We Know It* (New York, NY: Harper Business, 2000).

that smart." He later went on to jest that on his tombstone, it will be written that, "He was not that dumb, and he was not that smart."[14]

In all probability, none of your failures will likely reach this level of global scrutiny, but the point is that even a failure of this magnitude turned out to be a brilliant (if painful) decision in which they were actually able to snatch victory from the jaws of defeat. (I've had many experiences where people manage to do the opposite, firmly grabbing that failure in the midst of victory!)

A more humorous Coca-Cola story that I heard while living in Japan was about the incorrect translation of their slogan "Coke adds life" in China. The writing on their cans incorrectly said, "Coke brings back your dead ancestors!"[15]

May I have two cases, please? Or maybe three?

Handling Change

The only constant in life is change, even when we don't want it. Maybe especially then. I haven't been a huge fan of change, but I acknowledge the irony that change in my life has frequently led to better things and gotten me closer to my Holy Grail. It can still be frightening and unpleasant for the most part. Uncertainty is very closely linked to change for everyone; this can create fear, anxiety, or a sense of impending doom.

---

14. Kempner, "Keough an affable but tough Coke leader."

15. Christopher Klein, "Why Coca-Cola's 'New Coke' Flopped," History.com, updated September 14, 2023, https://www.history.com/news/why-coca-cola-new-coke-flopped.

I ask you to consider looking at change differently, as I've learned to do. That doesn't mean seeing it as an unqualified blessing because it's NOT. There are always pros and cons. But it's worth an open-minded exploration of the facts, the situation, and whether it will bring some benefits to you.

What's working? What's not? YOU must be willing to change if it makes you and your life better. It's another thing that's much easier said than done, but the rewards of doing it are abundant. Guided by that lovely saying, "Dance like no one is watching," try to take more ownership of your life, your well-being, and your future.

Conclusion

Early in your safari, you start to see the real hazards of the jungle, which aren't always the obvious ones. These can involve questions of morality, along with the complex tapestry of workplace competition, failure, reinvention, and change.

You'll see that pursuing a successful career involves dedication, effort, and sacrifice in terms of investing time and energy into education, prioritizing work over personal interest, and sometimes making difficult choices.

Chapter 4

"If You Got a Hunger for What You See, You'll Take It Eventually"

One of the key factors in your success is leadership. You can't become who you ultimately want to be if you're not a leader. You can make a lot of money, and you can still do amazing things. But in corporate America, and frankly, in so many aspects of our world, the people who make the biggest impact are true leaders. Leaders empower others to be their best selves and become leaders themselves.

Leadership is earned, not granted. And even when you're given a title that has leadership responsibility, it doesn't make you a leader, at least not a good or great one. That takes time, experiences, the ability to learn from those, and true empathy—the ability to put yourself in another's shoes, whether they're your boss's or a team member's.

When you're a leader, you recognize and empower people to be successful too. Sometimes that doesn't work out, but if it's part of your core, you'll be a real leader. Fundamentally, it quite simply comes down to caring about other people and using your skills to help them become even better future leaders, creators, or administrators. I didn't fully appreciate how much insight my early career experiences gave me, how they shaped my leadership style, and how early on you can exercise leadership, even if it's a simple issue.

There are opportunities we'll talk about that allow you to show your unique talents and have them stand on their own. At the same time, as you move up, be sure to extend the ladder down. Don't pull it up. As Michelle Obama perfectly stated, "When you walk through that doorway of opportunity, don't shut it behind you."[16]

Small Kindnesses Make a Massive Difference, Including Treats for the Boss

"For me, success is not about the wins and losses. It's about helping these young fellas be the best versions of themselves on and off the field."[17]

A wonderful recent example of the power of kindness and respect in life, in a career, and with a new boss can be found on the endlessly quoted television series *Ted Lasso* (starring the amazing Jason Sudeikis). When he begins his career as a football coach in the UK, he works for the owner, Rebecca. Each day, he brings her a box of special biscuits over her objections. Even as she protests, she's touched by this gesture and drives herself crazy trying to find out the source of the biscuits so she can get her own and not have to depend on Ted, who she doesn't really want to succeed in his role (not an unusual situation in any

---

16. The Wall Street Journal, "Michelle Obama: Door of opportunity," YouTube, September 4, 2012, https://www.youtube.com/watch?v=79CcOW7gM5g.

17. "How Ted Lasso's Leadership Lessons Made Me a Successful Leader," Build the Stage, buildthestage.com, July 19, 2021, https://www.buildthestage.com/how-ted-lassos-leadership-skills-made-me-a-successful-leader/.

occupation!). We discover later that he bakes these amazing biscuits himself each night to take to Rebecca. We see his innate goodness in this gesture, but we also understand that he gets human nature. The biscuits are his ticket to a relationship with someone who wants neither him nor any kind of relationship with him. It's strategic genius but also genuinely kind and simple. I'm not suggesting that you get out your apron and measuring cups each night—I simply wouldn't be able to without the risk of giving someone food poisoning. But you should pay attention to the silent cues and try to find your own magic for your biscuits.

Having a relationship with your boss (your immediate boss or supervisor) is always one of the most important factors in your success at a company. This relationship can be completely based on mutual trust and respect. It doesn't have to be a lifelong friendship or involve getting together on weekends, having lunch every day, or saying what they want to hear. Those things can be unhealthy. You can have a true friendship in some lucky circumstances, but it's rare and not the goal. The goal is for your boss to understand that YOU are a valuable member of the team. And you need to be willing to pay it forward with the people you work with, including said boss. That may take time, but if you stay the course, your work will be recognized. It can be more difficult if other people are between you and the ultimate boss, so if you listen and observe, an opportunity will present itself for you to be seen.

The little extras matter to anyone who has a pulse. You can never go wrong by being kind, being respectful, and taking an extra moment to connect with people in a genuine and authentic way.

I've always been told I'm too, well, everything. Too sensitive, too forgiving, too willing to sacrifice, too quiet, too loud . . . The list is endless. I no longer listen because I've seen the value and impact of what I've been criticized for. I genuinely love people, and although I recognize (and, at times, grieve for) what we're still going through, I believe we can get each other through the loss of family ties, the loss of faith in institutions, the problems created by social media, and the feelings of being more isolated, not less. After a global pandemic and turbulent political times, we're ALL learning how to be human again (and how to drive, but I digress), and some people have already failed that class.

But to be successful at any job, you must create connection, find your own support system, and create your own positive, healthy relationship with the boss and your team. There are so many things we have no control over. That knowledge in and of itself can be discouraging. We can control certain things WE do, how WE react, or things WE are responsible for, and we can use that to push forward incremental change. This isn't simply longing for a return of "Hope and Change" or wishing, praying, or dreaming. I've seen the power of these small things in the trajectory of my own career of over forty-five years. They DO matter, no question. I want to be remembered for my kindness and generosity, as well as the times I got it right and found just the perfect words. I want to be remembered for my grace in times of deep trouble and my struggle to do the right thing, even when it's the hard thing or the scary thing. I want to correct my mistakes and make amends where I can.

As I wrote portions of this book, I had a view of the office building where I had my first "real" (as opposed to entry-level, receptionist or intern) position and stayed for twenty-two years. It reminded me of thousands of moments of kindness and compassion I was blessed by and the many people who helped when they didn't need to, who gave an extra spark of recognition and exposed me to a fleeting sense of purpose, destiny even. For those who've gone ahead and live in my memories, I thank you with a gratitude that's endless. To those that are still on my safari, you have been amazing companions, and I am beyond grateful. I try to honor all of you by keeping your spirit and kindness alive or going and paying it back as much as possible in my life—by supporting and recognizing all those I can do the same for now, as well as acting as an ambassador for those issues I'm passionate about. One person can change the world. I've always believed this, and I always will.

Add Value

It's important to make sure your motives are aligned with the potential or existing clients/customers of whatever business you're in and of the firm/company. Whatever you're proposing must benefit THEM. It doesn't matter if you're the smartest, most fabulous, most charming person in the world. (And I'm sure you ARE, and I DO want to meet you!) But this doesn't mean your clients or colleagues care. You must determine what THEIR "why" is and how you can be part of their success, not just an expense or a necessity—and definitely NOT an obstacle in their path.

Listen carefully to find ways to solve problems they express in casual conversation that haven't yet made it to the action stage; it's a thinking-out-loud process. Whatever your special gifts are (we all have them)—numbers and math, reading the room, presenting, and more—find a way you can use this talent to contribute to future meetings, if not the one you're in. Watch the dynamics at play; people say and do fascinating things at times in meetings. Never (ever!) a dull moment.

Building Your Brand

If your future isn't important to you, who is it important to? You must be your own best advocate. Women, especially, are taught and subliminally trained to be modest, to not brag or toot our own horns. And it can be hard to figure out the best way to showcase their unique gifts while not being seen as bragging or delusional. And younger men are falling into the same trap of "How can I be seen?" without looking tone-deaf or unsure of how to promote themselves. The definition of what it means to be either or neither gender continues to reshape our world.

If you're paying attention to social media, you'll have noticed that almost everyone has decided to showcase themselves. Everyone has the right to shine their light in the world in whatever form they choose. But as part of the human family, I think we know we're bonded by the bad times as well as the good. There's tremendous value in reinforcing our connections and keeping in touch with special people who may be literally all over the world.

You can do whatever you want, but today more than ever, the world is watching. And it seems everyone is very motivated to be the star of their own life, which is fine and right. I would only urge some caution. You know that you find some of your friends' social media posts to be obnoxious. And there's a bit of curation and happiness inflation that's very human and natural. Try to keep it positive and uplifting but still real. And always remember that whatever you post lives FOREVER. Perhaps think twice or three times if there's any concern in your mind before you share with the world.

Giving Feedback and Receiving It: Good and Bad

You want people to tell you the truth. If they don't, they're actually hurting you. It's extremely difficult to give (and receive) feedback that's anything but positive and glowing with praise. And then there's reality. We all have weaknesses as well as strengths, and depending on where we intend to end up, we have to both understand and commit to addressing those weaknesses to succeed at the highest level. People don't want to deliver negative feedback or criticism because they don't want to hurt the other person, it's hard to deliver, they may fear retaliation or they may not be very good at it.

It's VERY easy to deliver happy news. Less-than-happy news, not so much. But you need to seek information about how you're performing so you can adjust and understand the perception of you and whether it matches your own view of the situation. It took me years to be able to receive negative or hard feedback, but it made me so much better and stronger once I was able to. The sooner you can hone this skill, the better it will be for the rest of your career. I still struggle to deliver negative feedback. That's another skill you might want to develop as early as possible; your life will be much easier.

Therefore, you must learn to hear, absorb, and process hard or negative feedback. And you must be willing to hear the things that may be holding you back. If your motivation to get better is strong enough, you'll find a way to make it okay to hear those things.

This has been one of my hardest lessons. It's very difficult to deal with negative feedback about ourselves. But one of the best things I can share with you is to be open to this and willing to hear it. You can't fix a problem you don't know you have. And you don't know what you don't know. I have stories about people who lost the opportunity to make their ultimate dream come true because the people around them didn't want to hurt or upset them, so they withheld negative feedback, resulting in the loss of achieving one or more most important life goals.

I've learned to better listen to and really hear all feedback (I don't think I'll ever master this). I've worked hard on this, both professionally and personally. I'm learning to listen more openly, honestly, and authentically to my adult son and my husband, as well as to the incredible people I work with and my friends. Most importantly, I want to know what I can do to be better at new stages in my life. It will be the same for you at work with your team and your people. In so many ways, we're as bonded as families are, and we owe each other honest and respectful dialogue. If we're going to spend all this time together and try to move mountains, shouldn't we also try to help each other find the metaphorical pot of gold in our lives?

I've tried to turn all feedback, good and bad, into an opportunity to make myself better and stronger and to open up doors that would have remained firmly closed if I hadn't been willing to be hurt, disappointed, and vulnerable. The best approach is captured in the phrase "Just Do It"—coined by that titan of the advertising world Dan Wieden (cofounder of Wieden+Kennedy), who famously created this slogan for his firm's first client, Nike, in 1988.

This is a lesson for EVERYONE. It doesn't matter who you are or what you are. We all feel unworthy and not good enough at times (some of us more frequently than others). It's hard to compete with both the negative voices in your head and the negative voices around you saying you can't or won't succeed. But you WILL. As you learn more about yourself and others around you, it gives you a deeper understanding, which nurtures your emerging skills and allows you to better succeed.

Good news, of course, is a relative walk in the park. When you receive it, be sure to be gracious and grateful. I'm not being patronizing in any way, honestly. When people support you and advocate for you, that's a gift. It doesn't always happen when it should, and I've found that people are more likely to help you again if you've shown that it matters to you, that you appreciate it, and that you're thrilled about your new raise, opportunity, promotion, or whatever wonderful news you got.

What's in a Title?

"It's not titles that honour men, but men that honour titles."[18]

Some titles are accurate, some aren't. Some are impressive, some aren't. You may love yours, or not. There's an almost Byzantine world of corporate titles. As you're in your observation phase, you'll have a chance to see what titles are bestowed and upon whom, as well as get a sense of what's expected and what it takes to climb the mountain. My personal plan in the early years was anything but cohesive, but it can be distilled in one word: *up*. That was my focus, rightly or wrongly. I wanted to keep growing, improving, taking on more responsibility, and, yes, getting paid more money. It was also a way for me to keep track (or even score) of how I was progressing.

---

18. Niccolò Machiavelli according to Philosiblog, "It is not titles that honor men, but men that honor titles." Philosiblog, January 28, 2012, https://philosiblog. com/2012/01/28/it-is-not-titles-that-honor-men-but-men-that-honor-titles/.

Every single new title or promotion I received was complicated and often a battle. Some of it was due to gender, some of it was due to a conflict with someone else's agenda, and some were fortuitous. You must fight for what you want, but ideally, you can't be seen as demanding, negative, needy. I say this not to be discouraging; I'm just sharing my observations of how senior leaders often think. I want you to get promoted! Once you get a certain title, you have some leeway in making the job your own, with your own special signature.

My most recent title is Vice Chair of the Pacific. I was promoted during the pandemic, at a time when we had major chaos, even beyond the fears for survival of our business, confusion about how to do our jobs (how many people lived on Zoom before?), and how to take care of people when you never see them. Because I'm in the insurance industry, I was also faced with one big question from clients, investors, major insurance carriers, etc.:

"Does insurance cover COVID?"

I could write a whole other book on this particular topic and likely will do so as a case study (although it will likely be far less interesting to most of you). But for our purposes, please know I was afraid that our whole business model might not last into the next decade, especially with climate change, clashing political ideologies, and global viruses without an identifiable etymology, path, overall risk, or damage. And that was just before 6:00 a.m.!

Receiving the title was almost like a tree falling in the forest, the sound heard by no one and creating no outward activity. It was spring of 2020, the relative beginning of a three-year (so far) global pandemic unlike anything that has been seen in a hundred years. We all worked remotely and only spoke on the phone or with very limited personal contact, so most people didn't even know I had a new role. I had to decide what my priorities should be, and it was incumbent on me to make it "real" and have it impact others positively. I was allowed the opportunity to take on more and define what I thought the priorities were for the Pacific region of the US, including DEI, strategic philanthropy, government relations, and legislation. For probably the first time in my entire career, by virtue of defining the role I believed was needed and what I should do, I got to write the script for my career, to a point, and I'm eternally grateful. I can't overstate that. When you're given those chances, make them count!

I began to test what would work and how to best relate to people in my new role while being mindful that I still had my existing role and responsibilities. I still very much needed to be there for my own clients and team while trying to help everyone.

However long it takes you, you can succeed in making a difference if your beliefs are strong and the need is powerful.

There's a mystique that does still exist in certain companies or certain positions and applies to entry to the most exclusive of spaces: the C-suite. The best definition of *C-suite* is that it refers to the most senior executives, most of whom have titles that tend to start with the letter *C*: chief executive officer, chief financial officer, chief operating officer, and chief information officer. It also includes the chair and vice chair, who, technically, represent the board of directors and to whom the C-suite theoretically reports. I'm the vice chair of the Pacific for my firm, and when a more junior associate was recently putting together a meeting with someone from our home office and the C-suite, I was excluded. The reason for this, I was told, was that my title "doesn't start with a *C*." Hmmm . . . I think that educating oneself on the rules that govern and determine board responsibilities (if nothing else, to prepare yourself for future opportunities) is a smart move.

One of my most important mentors and friends over my entire career recently took me to lunch and told me he was shocked that I made it to the C-suite. I reminded him that he'd always made me feel that he believed in me and told me to aim for the top. He quickly confirmed that yes, he did indeed always believe in me and saw something "extra." But being great and getting to the top are often two different things. Most people, even the extraordinary ones, never make it. And, while so many times I felt like I would fail or just crumble, on some level, I always knew I could achieve what I set my sights on—sometimes at great cost, sometimes by sheer luck, and often by meeting the moment, being willing to prepare as much as possible for the unknown, and taking the risk. And YOU can too.

When I shared the situation regarding the C-suite invitations with my friend, he texted his dad, a legendary titan of industry who's also a vice chair. I could almost hear the response through the phone as to whether he was sure he was in the C-suite as vice chair; the response might not lend itself to print. However, his dad's written works and speeches over the years have inspired me tremendously, including:

"Knowing what you don't know is more useful than being brilliant. Successful investing requires a certain kind of temperament . . . the ability to take losses and adversity without going crazy and an ability to not to be driven crazy by extreme success."[19]

Words to build a legend by!

---

19. Alice Judy, "The 71 Best Charlie Munger Quotes," AnQuotes.com, March 29, 2021. https://www.anquotes.com/charlie-munger-quotes/.

Getting Included in Meetings and What to Do When You're There

Getting to attend meetings that matter is one of your first goals. All too often, meetings aren't a place where things get done; sometimes, there really is a "room where it happened" (with apologies to Lin-Manuel Miranda's *Hamilton*), and it may be a while before you get in those. In the interim, it's important to figure out a way to be at meetings that truly further your growth and understanding. And once you get in the first one, it almost always creates additional opportunities to be in other meetings and gives you further credibility.

So, how do you get invited? You can express your interest to your boss or supervisor, of course, or even a colleague who's in the meeting who will advocate for you. You also might offer to add or bring something to the meeting that will benefit the group—organize the food, arrange the technology, do research that's needed, offer to discuss one topic, and be bulletproof when you prepare. All of these come to mind.

Earlier in your career, it's okay to be the designated notetaker. This is a time to embrace your inner teacher's pet and elevate the note-taking to a Pulitzer Prize-winning level. HOWEVER, all too often, either the only woman or one of the few women in the room gets asked to take notes. If, in fact, you're one of the more senior people in the room but the only *fill in the blank*—woman, minority, or LGBTQ+ person, for example—put your pen down, please, except for taking notes for your own use and reference. This is a disrespectful request. One wonders what you're supposed to do in these situations. Because we have a multigenerational workplace, it's even trickier (getting technical here!) to balance behavior, expectations, and responses. Since the meetings you want to be part of generally include clients, senior people, and/ or select peers, you're limited in your response options. However, stay present in the moment, make the best of things, use humor if appropriate, and later find a time to chat further with the person in charge of the meeting about your role and their expectations so you can better plan for future meetings. If their response is weak or doesn't give you comfort, you can elevate your concerns after trying a bit longer to see if they heard you and made changes.

For young men, especially if there are women in the room, you will make a wonderful impression if you assist with some things that are typically delegated or expected to be done by women (e.g., take notes, help with refreshments). It will be noticed and admired. Of course, you should also focus on helping in areas where you are strong—the technology, the topic or timing.

One of the truly puzzling moments in my career came from someone in London I thought was my friend and who was an important trading partner of mine. They asked me to bring their tea and to be sure "it's the way you know I like it," thereby designating me as coffee girl, not leader, and elevating themselves. The meeting was with the chairman of a very important client. This was after the person had stolen my presentation ideas for this particular client, including hours of research and my learned experience, which I'd unwisely mentioned prior to the meeting. They took my ideas and presented them as theirs, gaining the respect of the key decision-maker. This was followed by ordering me to get their tea "as per usual." Clearly, this was disrespectful and intentionally rude, but karma is real, and I was able to observe the consequences. Tea, anyone? May I have almond milk and sugar? You know the way I like it.

Expectations (Including Unspoken) of Your Role at a Meeting, Meal, or Event

While you should never let anyone take advantage of you, it might be helpful to recognize that earlier in your career, your time has less value than that of the more senior folks on the team. I still do whatever it takes when it comes to making a meeting or an event extra special. I'll scrub the toilet at the venue and refresh the potpourri basket (did that last year on a major client trip). It's about the experience in its totality—the ability to step back and break down the successful outcome into its component parts. It really does have value. It matters, and I'm only offering guidance based on how we conduct these events with various levels of seniority—the client's and our firm's—and my thoughts are based on what I've seen work well. If you see something, say something, and not just at airports regarding suspicious packages. You can make yourself more valuable as an observer who can see things that perhaps your boss or others can't. They're often reacting in the moment or focused on what they're going to be saying or doing, so they can miss some of the unspoken dynamics that give more insight into what's really going on than mere words would.

Look around the room. Is everyone engaged? Does someone need someone to talk to? Do they need a drink or guidance to their seat? (Even Katy Perry had a tough time with that one at the coronation of King Charles III.) And what's the overall mood? Are you picking up on any tension? Can you do anything that enhances the positive vibes you're feeling? Or can you redirect any negative tones? This isn't to suggest that the emotional state of everyone present is your responsibility. But observation and the ability to read a room are incredibly valuable skills that truly help the situation, the team, and YOU.

Remember, you're in this alone, as, indeed, we all are in life. Yes, you may have the blessings of a great family, friends, or team, or you might not at times. It's on you to take care of you. It's neither fair nor unfair. It's just reality. So don't let anyone hurt you or try to take you down. This is MUCH easier said than done, but you can learn how to protect yourself and your spirit. Surround yourself when you can with people who bring out your best, and make time for them to nourish your spirit—the family, the team, the childhood and college friends, and new friends. All are welcome. We all need a circle (or a village) to help us navigate difficult terrain. Stay in shape physically—getting sick makes everything twice as hard. Stay sharp mentally—have outside interests that have nothing to do with your work but center you and keep your brain sharp.

You have a world to change! Please take my hand, and we'll move forward!

Opportunities for Promotion

Almost every type of organization (including but not limited to for-profit, not-for-profit, military, volunteer, and government) has a system of job titles that include salary ranges and other benefits as you go (presumably) up in the organization. Where are you on the sometimes mysterious and often opaque ladder in your situation? Are you feeling challenged and rewarded? What titles do you aspire to?

Within reason (but not always the case in the past!), you generally must do what you're asked to do. If you're being asked to do things that are wrong or off, it may be time for a change. In other words, if someone you report to asks you to do something that feels inappropriate or just like a really bad approach, you can question the reason for the request to clarify your understanding or get a better idea of the rationale for future situations. If, after discussion, there isn't really a valid reason, this is a reason to be concerned. My reaction to those situations is to wait and see. Is this an outlier, or an unusual behavior or request? If, after you give it a little time, you decide that it's not, you may want to work with someone else or transfer. If this behavior is more the rule than the exception, it's probably time to look at leaving.

Conclusion

You're building the foundations of your career and life. We've explored the bricks that constitute your pivotal early steps, including developing leadership skills (never too early or too late to work on these). These should be authentic to your style and beliefs. YOU are the architect of your career. We've also looked at strategies for showcasing your talents, understanding the expectations others will have of you, and getting included in important meetings and projects.

Constantly learning is a gift and an opportunity available to all of us. This can be a joyful, lifelong habit that will benefit you in countless ways that, for now, seem to lie in a very distant future. You're armed with your natural gifts and some additional tools now. Let's keep it moving—forward!

Chapter 5

"You Can Have Anything You Want, But You Better Not Take It from Me"

Understanding some of the ways in which other people can and may harm you or try to hold you back helps you. Everyone has their own reasons for their behavior. Some people truly value collaboration; others seem to thrive on competition. There are some gender dynamics at play in today's workplace, along with many other issues that impact behavior. You need tools to be able to identify, manage, and, if possible, eliminate the behavior, minimize contact, or use it to your advantage.

Zero-Sum Game

Somehow, we've allowed this narrative to prevail in our workplaces, our communities, and our world. It's a false belief that for me to win, you must lose. There are, of course, circumstances where this could be true, which complicates things further. This isn't going to change without all of us trying to reset the narrative. And it can be counter to human nature and self-interest to make those changes. Some people don't want a win-win culture or to support one. But do you REALLY want to hold other people back? Assume that your well-being and success aren't impacted by anyone else. So, in this hypothetical scenario, you're not competing for scarce resources, or the same job, or whatever it is. Wouldn't you wish for every person to find some measure of peace, safety, and security, if not happiness?

How Colleagues Can Undermine You

Those lovely folks you work with can be allies or adversaries. When it works, it's a beautiful thing. It's hard to beat collaboration and camaraderie. But when it doesn't, it can feel like being dropped into a pit of scorpions. There are some classic ways your colleagues, team members, and even bosses can undermine you for their own purposes. This is the exception, not the rule, in my experience. But it happens with enough frequency that you'll need to expect it and prepare for it. There are a number of typical ways that your work family can become something out of a Grimms' fairy tale.

Rumors and Innuendo

It is easier to tear down a reputation than build one. I've observed countless times over the years where a whispered or suggested comment can become fact very quickly—especially if it's not true or only a tiny bit true—through gossip and repeated affirmations. Innuendo and speculation are way more appealing than boring facts. I've been the subject of a false narrative only a few times, but it's painful, and it can be truly toxic. We see it discussed in the media as part of cancel culture or the loss of the belief that someone is innocent until proven guilty.

With the grace and kindness of the universe, I was able to find opportunities to affirmatively address the talk in a series of meetings, and I was armed with facts and proof of false statements. That was a tough one, and it took me many years to acquire the skill to do. You may not get the opportunity to correct misinformation, certainly not in real time and possibly not online (I'm hoping it doesn't get to an online situation because that's a whole other level, I know). I had to be humble when I was angry, non-blaming (when I totally blamed some of the people), and conciliatory when I was anything but. But the noise went away. And if I hadn't dealt with it, I would have lost meaningful opportunities for the future, which were much more important. You have to correct the narrative, repudiating false facts either affirmatively or through your behavior.

On one of the points of misinformation, I later heard some people say, "We can't count on her 100 percent because of her health." So, even if you die, you aren't good enough. And people always pick up a thread of truth and weave it into a poncho.

Remember that you're responsible for protecting yourself from other people, whether they're not observing your boundaries, behaving in a destructive way, or actively seeking (even in a secretive way) to harm you and your career.

Socializing and Building Relationships

Human beings are social animals. We're born wired for connection, as we discussed. It's literally in our DNA. People often refer to their colleagues as their "work friends," or their "work family," or "the team." And there are so many benefits from having positive, supportive relationships in the workplace. This is important to you because you'll feel a greater sense of purpose, you won't feel alone, and you'll have a greater connection to the organization. You'll have people to rely on when you have a problem or a crisis.

Looking ahead in your career and channeling Spider-Man for a moment, "With great power, comes great responsibility." Or said another way, with a biblical influence, "To whom much is given, much will be required" (Luke 12:48). The point is that we're part of the human continuum and experience, and if you're blessed with gifts of talent, intellect, wealth, knowledge, time, or other gifts (and we all bring different gifts to the table at different times in our lives), you may want to take a moment to reflect on your own power, your values, and your choice to share your gifts to make the world a better place. When you're the mentee, it's not too soon to be thinking about how you would be as a mentor. This will both make your time with your mentor more impactful and help you hone your own coaching skills.

Cultivating the Right Relationship with the Appropriate Executives

There's your supervisor/boss, and there's often the team leader, the department or practice leader, and on up to the C-suite executives. It's important to ultimately have a chance to meet or show your stuff in front of the "big" (which can be a relative term) boss(es). But most of your happiness and fate will be determined by your immediate boss/supervisor.

Hopefully, you'll work with someone great who does want to help you succeed and grow. But the road to a successful career is often littered with bad bosses. (That's part of the reason so many movies and television shows riff on this stereotype.) If you do win the boss lottery, it will be easier for you to learn, feel a sense of belonging, and find your path.

However, it is possible to navigate a situation where you truly don't like the person, or you don't respect them, or, even worse, they don't like or respect you. But it's a challenge. I've had this experience many (too many) times. It's probably the main reason people leave jobs that they otherwise like or feel have great potential. If you have a support system at home or with colleagues or family, you can withstand a fairly long run with a bad boss. I'm encouraged that for those now entering the jungle, there are additional options and protections that you have (I know it doesn't always feel like it!) compared to how trapped I was at times. As we've discussed, adversaries can be great teachers too. I'm not a victim, and you already know that I share the belief that everyone who enters your life, for good or bad, has a purpose or a lesson that can teach you or inspire you. This reminds me of what my mom and my aunties from the South believe.

We continue to talk about the importance of balance. In any relationships or events at work, you want to be mindful of keeping things in the proper space. You want your boss to see you as someone who's a team player with certain key skills, some unique to you, all valuable. But you don't need them to see you at 2:00 a.m. showing off your coolest dance moves from high school or college.

Mentorship

Almost everyone who makes it to the top has a mentor or several mentors along the way. There are definitely advantages to finding mentors, but there are also some things to be wary of.

Mentorship must be organic to be authentic. It's a very real connection between two people, and it's a two-way street.

You want to know how to find a mentor. Some companies have formal mentorship programs, but in my experience, those are rarely successful. There may be some short-term benefits, and the recognition of the need and the attempt to solve for it are commendable. But over the long run, I feel it's an inauthentic solution. Only you will know who you feel most comfortable talking to and taking advice from. It may take time to figure that out, and it's fine. You don't want to have a mentor who's a bad fit because you were checking off a list. It will happen, I promise, and it will develop out of a positive, healthy working relationship. What YOU can do is be open to opportunities to work with different people, express an interest in working on certain projects, ask questions (thoughtful ones, if you can), and volunteer. Back to the knowledge discussion—keep learning as much as you can so you'll know the people who are the smartest or the most talented at certain things. Then you'll have a better sense of who can genuinely help you. (There may be more than one person, and at various points in your career, you may have different mentors as you need to learn different skills.)

Sometimes, when the mentor/mentee are of different genders (however you or circumstances choose to define that), there are other elements at work. Because I came up in a different era, my best mentors were men. Many of them were incredible, truly changed my life, and remain close friends. (Senior women of the time were few and far between, and there was an unspoken rule not to help each other; it was truly a zero-sum game.)

However, there were a few who seemed to believe I was beholden to them for imbuing me with the rare gift of their wisdom and needed to somehow balance the scale. This wasn't my view of things, but I really had no recourse other than to avoid, deflect, be funny, and be able to run fast. For anyone who puts others in that situation or takes advantage of anyone's youth, inexperience, or need to learn from you, there's a special place in Hell waiting on your arrival.

Everyone has an agenda. An agenda isn't inherently bad. I've tried to be a truly good mentor. I do leave my ego outside the room in conversations, and I genuinely want to help people for the sake of leaving a legacy of love and light, as well as to live the life I've always wanted by being the person I've always wanted to be.

To wander for a moment to the developmental psychology behind both our needs in life and the purpose of a mentor, I wish to refer to the solid science of the old Maslow's Hierarchy of Needs. This theory, proposed by Abraham Maslow, states that there's a five-tier model of all human needs—a triangle, if you will—with the physiological needs (food, water, air, sleep, shelter, clothing) at the bottom and rising up the triangle in this order: safety, love/belonging, esteem, and self-actualization.[20]

This illustrates the theory, which is as true today as when Maslow first introduced it in 1943, that you must be secure in your ability to house, clothe, and feed yourself before you can address any of your emotional/psychological needs. So, when we're starting out, we're often (understandably) focused on how to pay the rent, pay for gas, buy clothes and food, and maybe go out once or twice.

As we become more secure financially and feel like we can provide our basic needs for ourselves, we're able to start to look at our lives in

---

20. Saul Mcleod, "Maslow's Hierarchy of Needs Theory," Simply Psychology, updated October 18, 2023, https://www.simplypsychology.org/maslow.html.

their totality. The top, or the final, tier of human discovery is the self-actualization piece. Everything you're doing now or will do in the future on your journey leads to this place. It's the culmination of your life in some ways while still leaving the important questions for closer to the end.

Legacy is a key component of self-actualization. Did I make a difference? Did I matter while I was here in the cosmic blink of an eye? As people achieve the basics for a safer, more secure life, they do have the luxury of thinking about purpose and, yes, legacy. How will I be remembered? Did I use my hard-earned wisdom to benefit others? Was I a mentor? A teacher? A coach? A friend? These thoughts and what they represent become so much more powerful as you get older.

If you can find a way to work on the top while still climbing, it's a worthwhile thing to do. The young can also mentor the older. My son often gives me advice on business issues from a perspective that I wouldn't have otherwise, and it makes a huge difference. Sometimes we feel the pain of loss and disappointment on the climb, but it all results in our growth and coming closer to our true purpose and ultimate joy.

There may come a time when the student surpasses the master. This is part of normal evolution, and it's a tribute to the master. (I've been a faithful student, and I've tried to be a wise master and let the student find their own brilliance.) But as with many parents and children, this can be a tough transition. When you're the student surpassing the master, this takes particularly skillful maneuvering. And when you're the master and see the student take the leap, it's best to STAY OUT OF THE WAY and applaud them. You aren't in it for the gratitude. You're there for all the right reasons and to use your power for good. You'll be recognized (or possibly not). It won't be on your timetable (as with parenting!), but it's just the sprinkles on your sundae or granola.

There's enormous satisfaction and power from knowing you helped someone else become a better version of themselves. It's the greatest gift you can give anyone. You also receive a gift: knowing you used your power for good and made a positive difference in the life of another human being. It gives you a chance to see things in another way and make changes to yourself that may now be right and beneficial. You also have a chance to check your own compass and see if you're going in the right direction. That's a win by any metric.

Competition with Men for Women

The workplace dynamic between genders has evolved and changed during my career.

In my earliest days, a newly hired woman (and all the inside office jobs were filled by women, just as all the executives were male) inadvertently triggered my awareness of my second-class status. The new woman's name was Jeanine. (The things you do remember!) She asked me if any of the other women objected to being given household labor tasks each Monday to complete. Duties included washing all dishes, dusting the furniture, making coffee throughout the day, and cleaning the owner's and other principal's private bathroom (toilet included—fun times!). No men were ever given any of these tasks, no matter what their level. I remember blurting out, "You mean we have a choice?" So intense was my internalized message of having to be a "good girl"—meaning not speaking out, not pushing back, not making a fuss—that I was truly puzzled by her question. I can still remember the look of genuine pity she gave me for accepting my treatment.

And she didn't even know all the assignments that were given to me. For example, I had to find a suitable piece of jewelry for the boss's girlfriend but NEVER allow any information to get to his wife. There was an implicit assumption that I would enable the owner's adultery, but no one ever asked me if I was okay with this. Oh, and there was this bizarre fish tank in the owner's office with highly prized exotic fish that were extremely delicate and had to be kept alive at all costs. The fish were valued and treated better than the women who worked for him and helped him build his millions. We were required to arrive early and stay late to complete all these tasks, and we didn't receive any extra pay for this, which I believe was illegal, even at that time. If I wasn't willing to do any of these things, there was a very long line of people who would be happy to adjust to his morality and dust, scrub, and polish every area of his office, and even his life.

This was a recurring theme in my career. I was no one special. There were many others who could replace me. The other women were helpful to me; they were endlessly patient while I learned a new subject, one that turned out to open a lifetime of opportunity to me. But they had the same dilemma I did.

So, when I started my safari, competing with men wasn't an option because women were openly categorized and accepted as second-class citizens. Competing with men is something I've gradually learned to do and have done regularly. But given the rules of the game when I began, I wasn't sure if I ever could. And I'm not sharing these stories because I'm old and nostalgic, but rather because I'm genuinely concerned that as certain personal freedoms and civil liberties are eroded, we could go backward. I want younger generations to understand that those were not happy, wonderful times; there was basically little or no diversity, and women couldn't even express a desire to challenge a man for a position. And while it was great for the young men of those times, young men today don't have this advantage anywhere near how it was then. (Of course, it should be equal now.) But they're still viewed as having the advantage and are getting lost in the jungle. We must keep moving forward, and we appear to be frozen in place.

My career's beginning was the norm for women at the time. If you really tried to stop the madness, it was unlikely that anything would change, and you would be penalized and lose everything you'd accomplished. How many people would you risk your career for?

A partial explanation for why these circumstances continued for so long in the workplace can be found in the lose-lose proposition that was brought into focus during the days of Rosie the Riveter. Rosie was an allegorical cultural icon representing the brave women who worked in factories and shipyards during World War II to fill jobs that were previously done by the men who, by and large, were serving in the military.

Rosie was personified in song and film and on posters that were enormously successful in raising feelings of patriotism and gave women a new sense of purpose.

As World War II ended and the menfolk returned home, it was clear they wanted their old lives back to put distance between themselves and the war. Women were told that the vital duties they'd performed were "unnatural" and that the country needed a return to "normalcy." Thus, the opportunity to include women in a booming post-war economy was squandered, but the embers of a greater revolution were lit. In addition, the issue of childcare reared its head, as it does. During the war, women formed groups to share childcare duties, cooking, and shopping, and they found an effective approach like that of women and children in prehistoric times, when the proverbial village cared for the young as a sacred and communal duty. But no. Just no. In 1944, as victory seemed assured for the Allies, government propaganda began the push to return women to their proper place in the home.

One movie that I feel captures the emotion and zeitgeist of the moment is *A League of Their Own*, directed by Penny Marshall in 1992, with an amazing cast including Geena Davis, Tom Hanks, Lori Petty, Madonna, and Rosie O'Donnell. It showed us the essence of the conflict then and now (the baseball setting is a perfect metaphor). Should women be allowed to chase their dreams and fulfill their potential or be forced to choose between that and their families? It was a critical and commercial home run, shattering the myth that female-centric movies can't be profitable. Also, in 2012, the Library of Congress selected it for preservation in the National Film Registry as "culturally, historically or aesthetically significant."

A former male colleague of mine from a prior firm (Johnson & Higgins, a privately owned insurance broker that made it to the top of their game and their industry, only to sell to a large public company) joined my current firm after I'd been there for five years. This person was a man from a very privileged background, went to Stanford, and was very plugged into the Los Angeles elite and my industry. He looked like a cover model for *GQ*. It was understood from the moment he walked in as a summer intern right before his senior year of college that he had an unrestricted path to glory. And he was one of dozens there. When he was given an intimidating number for revenue he was expected to bring in, he said, "Of course I can do that. If Teena can do it, anyone can." Since he said it very loudly in front of me at a dinner, I felt like he'd thrown food at me or done something equally outrageous. But it was still not considered appropriate for me to respond or call out his disrespect. (This was about eighteen years ago.) As he bragged about his rolodex and how he was going to bring in this massive revenue, I felt vaguely queasy. I was doing well, and almost all of my clients had followed me over from my prior firm (which I feel very blessed by and grateful for), and I had a modest growth plan. But once again, I was up against someone who had advantages I just didn't. My son was very young, so I was also a working mom and was being pulled in a thousand directions. He was divorced and didn't have custody of his kids, so he had lots of time to invest in the business. Except that the people from his rolodex didn't want to do business with him, and he didn't really work all that hard after all. But his tan was truly a work of art. Best EVER.

He resigned after three years, just ahead of being fired, and he never duplicated my achievements. Turns out that in the end, you actually need to do the work in addition to looking the part!

For young men, it was historically easier to get support and mentorship from senior men in a firm/company, but now, there are many senior women also, and there's a bit of hesitation about how exactly to mentor young men and integrate opportunities between women and men. There are some parallels between that and what I experienced early in my career when women were the less desirable candidates or leaders. I believe, in case it wasn't clear before, that we ALL have a responsibility to mentor, teach, and provide opportunities for ALL young people of ALL genders. Senior women now have an obligation to mentor young men also. As mentioned, my mentors in my early career were almost all male, and I don't want to ignore young men when male leaders did not ignore me as a young woman. But women still need help getting to the very top of organizations. We can accomplish two things at once; just as one can hold two contradictory ideas in your mind.

Younger generations are certainly changing the landscape on this, but up to now, men were mostly winning. And when I look at an imaginary movie of my current firm, men still hold most of the power. I can certainly attest that it isn't the right approach not to have diversity in leadership. We all talk a lot about how powerful diversity is, but for most of corporate America, we don't really see it at the very top or when the most critical decisions are made. I struggle with the fact that over the years, even though I'm in the room, my feedback is sometimes ignored. I'm no longer quiet and uncertain, so it takes work to ignore me. And the stakes are high because many critical decisions have an outsized impact on people. As I've said, I very much believe that men and women and different generations are much stronger together almost all the time. However, we must create an intentional mindset where we recognize and understand that there will be conflicts, disagreements, and very different perspectives. So, you must agree to listen, not demand total agreement from each other, and seek common ground that supports the ultimate objective.

And as we continue to observe, young men are struggling, and we see fewer interns and entry-level folks from that group. I'm concerned about how that plays out into the future. That's the caveat to the "men winning" narrative. We're at risk of losing a generation of young men while some people seek to further limit a woman's freedom. It's a dark moment in history if one is paying close attention, set against a concerning backdrop of political tribalism.

I believe that any formula that makes $2 + 2 = 5$ instead of $2 + 2 = 3$ is a victory. These mathematically incorrect and somewhat exaggerated formulas are to illustrate a point that you can create a scenario where the whole is LESS than the sum of its parts, or it can be MORE.

We're all looking for purpose beyond providing for ourselves and our families. (Although, without being able to do that, everything else is secondary.) We can achieve this, but it absolutely takes work, dedication, and the desire for a better outcome.

Competition with Women

When I began my journey, and speaking from the viewpoint of a woman, there were almost no women who were actual leaders. The highest level of anyone I interacted with was vice president (one) and a few assistant vice presidents (the title where the few women who made it would spend the rest of their careers). Most of the junior and senior women wanted the same thing the rest of us did, so they often sought to neutralize us. They were the worst competitors. There was an unspoken rule (and several of my friends who identify as minorities have shared that they also felt this way): "The firm will only hire, promote, or invest in a few of us (whatever *us* represents), so I need to step over you to secure my position."

Thankfully, that's no longer the case. Throughout my career, I've always had wonderful relationships with clients who were women. It was an interesting contrast, almost head-spinning. And gradually, as more and more women joined the ranks of corporate America at all levels, including leadership roles, it began to change. I saw women supporting each other actively and affirmatively. Of all the things that have occurred over the course of my career, that's one that truly fills my heart with joy and pride.

I was once told women in business tended to have the "crab mentality." If you ever have a chance to observe crabs or lobster in a bucket after they've been caught and are now hanging out on the dock, you may note that some intrepid and motivated crabs will purposefully and confidently try to climb out. Some get out, but others feel themselves pulled back down into the bucket by some of their crab "friends." And they, too, are trapped. I have worked very hard to change this behavior and mindset, and I am hopeful that change is coming.

The crustaceans you may know and perhaps trust are bound and determined to keep you down with them. It's kind of the cliché, "If I can't get free to live my life, neither can anyone else." And even a bit of "Misery loves company." It's part of a far more complicated social order that happens to living things when they're threatened or given limited options for survival. We see this play out throughout all levels of an organization and in so many areas of our lives.

For young men starting out in the jungle, it can be much harder today than the experiences of men of prior generations. The historical advantages men have had are not necessarily true for the current generation. Not all senior women are willing to mentor young men (which I do NOT agree with), and young women who are competing with you seem to be more empowered and more confident, and they also seem to be receiving favorable treatment. Yes, it's the inevitable swing of the pendulum, but as always, the pendulum overcorrects and creates new problems. I am hopeful that things will eventually level and equalize, and I am working toward that end.

As the world has changed and organizations evolved, phrases like "toxic work environment" and "bullying" are more common; at the same time there is more being done to stop some of the historically destructive behavior and sabotaging that has gone on for years. And I do think that the current generations of millennials and Gen Z have so many things right about true inclusion, fairness, and refusal to accept the old rules and behavior. Thank God. As torches are passed, I believe we'll see more progress and less open warfare, but there are so many new challenges to worry about—the role of AI, climate change, the possibility of another global pandemic, social isolation, challenges of remote work, and the real estate market, to name a few that we're currently dealing with. There's more emphasis on collaboration and less of a zero-sum mentality. But it still will take time for the old behaviors to die, and as we've seen, they may be replaced with even greater problems. Each generation has its own journey and legacy to define.

Men and Women Working Together

Until we as women stop judging and attacking each other's choices, we can't move forward with equal rights and opportunities. And until men willingly accept additional responsibilities of being a parent and/or a team player at home, same goes.

Countless studies have shown that children with loving, involved fathers are significantly more likely to do well in school, have higher self-esteem, exhibit empathy and pro-social behavior, and avoid high-risk behaviors. A child who has the loving support of BOTH parents[21] is a true winner, and we owe that to our children.

---

21. Jennifer E. Lansford, "The Importance of Fathers for Child Development," Psychology Today, June 15, 2021, https://www.psychologytoday.com/us/blog/parenting-and-culture/202106/the-importance-fathers-child-development.

This isn't an issue solved by holding moms back and making them solely responsible. That solution hurts both parents equally. It forces a mom to give up her possible dreams of success outside her role as mother and creates (sometimes) resentment and burnout, as normal outlets, like having lunch with friends and getting dressed up, etc., are harder to do or plan. And for dads, they miss the absolute joy that comes from unstructured time with their precious baby. It really is a WIN-WIN if you can strive for (and it's not easy, and it's never equal) equal partnership in all things home, work, and parenting.

There's no ONE way to parent or live your life. If there were, all humans would be perfect, and no one would be unhappy or confused. Let's stop hurting each other with the noise of criticism and the pain caused by judgment at home and at work.

Building a Team or a Tribe (And Who to Lie Down on the Tracks For)

Over time, you'll have the opportunity to have one person, several, or many reporting to you. In the beginning, you're a member of the team, and you still have obligations to the team to support and mentor each other. It's the reason many people refer to their work colleagues as their "work family." It's also the beginning of learning how to lead.

I've had the privilege of being mentored over the years by several amazing men and women, and I'm forever in their debt. They literally gave me this career through the gift of their wisdom and their patience in teaching me what I needed to know when I needed to know it. There are many who also showed me how NOT to be helpful or to be anything resembling a mentor. They're long forgotten.

Leadership is the top trait or characteristic that's most in demand in all organizations—(and indeed the world—now). Part of leading is being strong enough and wise enough to support YOUR people. That's those who do a lot of the work and help you succeed. You owe them mutual loyalty and support as well as recognition. Do NOT be a glory hog. You WILL become bacon if you do so.

More importantly, being someone's champion, especially someone particularly deserving, is its own reward. If you care about people and invest your time in training them and learning from them, it's your sacred duty to mentor them, help them find the path forward, and help them be a better version of themselves. You won't regret it. It's part of your payment to the universe. It's also part of your humanity to repay those who give you their time, their work, and their trust. Especially if their efforts help you be more successful, you need to help them be successful too. Some examples of sharing credit are when someone compliments you on a successful project, and you affirmatively say you couldn't have done it without Susie's or Jack's help and that they really are without peer on this topic. Show and tell in this situation. And don't feel that when you share credit or give the credit that's due, it will diminish you in some way. Simon Sinek said, "A star wants to rise to the top. A leader wants to see others rise to the top."[22]

The founder of my present firm, Jack Lockton, had a saying: "It's no fun to drink champagne alone." Order a couple cases; celebrate, everyone!

---

22. Simon Sinek according to GoodreadsQuotes.com, "A star wants to see himself . . ." Goodreads Quotes, accessed October 22, 2023, https://www.goodreads.com/quotes/669905-a-star-wants-to-see-himself-rise-to-the-top.

Colleagues (Good and Bad)

According to Jean-Paul Sartre in *No Exit*, "*L'enfer, c'est les autres*" ("Hell is other people").

Yep, Sartre got it right. Hell can indeed be other people. Heaven can also be other people. (And so can purgatory!). Sometimes, we have freedom to choose, and sometimes we don't.

Robert Fulghum wrote, "Everything I need to know about life, I learned in kindergarten."[23] I might add, "In elementary and high school too!" The schoolyard sandbox is still alive and well as a metaphor for working in an office. There's a reason a show cleverly named *The Office* resonated with so many people. It's a universal experience of life—from day care groups for babies to kindergarten and beyond, and through all levels of education, joining a volunteer organization, or taking a new job in a big company. It's all the same issue of finding a way to belong to a new group. The behaviors we develop from our early childhood follow us throughout our lives, even when we're not aware that we're defaulting to them. Understanding the origin of some of our feelings, reactions, and responses is precious knowledge. It also gives us great insight into others in our workplace.

Some of Fulghum's rules for a successful life that he found in kindergarten include:[24]

- Play fair.
- Don't hit people.

---

23. Robert Fulghum according to Goodreads, Goodreads Quotes, accessed October 2, 2023, https://www.goodreads.com/quotes/246075-these-are-the-things-i-learned-in-kindergarten-1-share.

24. Fulghum according to Goodreads, Goodreads Quotes.

- Clean up your own mess.
- Don't take things that aren't yours.
- Live a balanced life.
- Warm cookies and cold milk are good for you.

That last one is important. Please pass the chocolate chips!

Even in the jungle, everyone comes at the end of the day to the watering hole. Zebras sip their water side by side while cautiously glancing at the elephants and giraffes, and everyone is on guard and avoiding the lions. I mean no disrespect to my colleagues or anyone else's by comparing them to our magnificent friends in the animal kingdom who gather together for essential things but still maintain their own purpose, along with healthy trepidation about the encounters. Some of our behavior is primal, instinctive, and shared across all creatures. That doesn't mean the zebra is joining the lions for cocktails and s'mores at the end of the night. In fact, I can almost guarantee that will not be happening.

I watched a motivational speech by Ray Lewis, the former American football champion who's now a philanthropist and activist. It was almost custom-made for this book; he talked about lions interacting with hyenas and zebras, or rather, NOT.

His point is that "a lion never negotiates with a hyena, and lions don't go to the club with the zebras."[25] He says there are two types of people—those who make things happen and those who watch things happen. You need to hang out with the people who inspire you to do more. Choose now and choose wisely, and don't be afraid to make different choices or adjust as you grow and evolve.

---

25. Magnum Motivation, "Lion Mentality | One of the Best Speeches Ever by Ray Lewis - Powerful Motivational Speech [4K]," YouTube, February 21, 2021, https://www.youtube.com/watch?v=uMTO1GtUy.

Conclusion

We've seen how many dimensions competition has and how complex it can be, although most companies now are highlighting the importance of creating inclusive environments that foster collaboration and utilization of everyone's specific skills and gifts. And yet, toxic conditions are still very much with us, and they're detrimental to all.

Leaders play an important part by fostering a culture that celebrates healthy competition, which can increase performance, innovation, and a healthy, thriving workplaces for all.

Chapter 6

"You're Going to Bleed, But It's the Price You Pay. I Want to Hear You Scream."

Pursuing a successful career involves dedication, effort, and sometimes difficult choices. It could mean sacrifices in terms of investing time and energy into education, prioritizing work over personal interests in the short term, or forgoing immediate gratification for future rewards. It's also a time for you to refine your own goals, beliefs, and code of ethics. It takes time to become the person you're meant to be. And back to our friend Coach Ted Lasso, "Believe." Do believe in yourself because I believe in you. You've GOT this, and time will polish brass to a beautiful patina, sparkles into brilliance, and fear into an ally. I promise. But you have to SURVIVE first. I would love to be your guide in the wild. I have another sign in my office (yes, I'm a visual person, motivated by things I see) that says, "Be Strong. Be Free. Be True. Be You." Yep, just do it!

Nothing worthwhile is easy. Or, as my daddy used to say, "Talk's cheap. It takes money to buy whiskey." He also said often, "I can't promise you that life will ever be fair, but it will always be interesting." You were so right, Daddy! We often trap ourselves in false beliefs or narratives, and only we can set ourselves free.

Passive Resistance

As we're all returning to or entering a brave new world, I believe this is an opportunity to gain new insight, look at boundaries, reshape the conversation, and ultimately find a way to help everyone. Ways to create these benefits include being more intentional about spending time in the office and scheduling coffee, lunch, meals, or snacks (whatever works) with team members, clients, or mentors. We all have the excuse of having been away from the world and, indeed, civilization for three years (with the exception of the incredibly brave folks who were out and about on the front lines during COVID-19 and may have PTSD from their time), and it's a one-time excuse that will allow bridges to be built or wounds to be healed by acknowledging this and giving others grace. Although communicating via text, email, or social media is one approach, I would suggest trying to substitute IRL (in real life) time with as many people as you can. This helps you sharpen your interpersonal skills, lets people know you care about them, and makes room for the energy and detail that comes from being together and talking live and in person.

However, not everyone is happy to be back, nor are they all ready to reignite and reinvent themselves or anyone or anything. There's a bit of passive resistance at play in the current moment. I would define this as the behavior of others when they're unwilling or unable to help you, but they don't disclose this fact or the reasons for it.

Back in your office, when you're trying to get someone to help you on a project, work with you on a client, or teach you how to do something (again, I learn at least one new thing a day, even when I REALLY do not want to!), you may encounter friction and an unwillingness to work with you or help you.

YOU have new opportunities for engagement and empowerment and to find more sense of purpose (which, as we've discussed at length, we all need and flourish from).

At work, you may also be blamed and cited as the reason for the unwillingness of others to engage with you. You need to listen (even when you don't want to) with an open mind and, even if you disagree, keep your mouth closed in the beginning. We can all have very different views of the same event or issue; it's incumbent on us to find the solution if we want to find the win.

Pain Threshold for Microaggressions/Abusive Behavior

There has been a lot of discussion surrounding microaggressions. What are they actually? Recognizing the state of the world we live in, we seem to be an angrier society than ever before. I write this in late 2023 as we're still emerging, like shell-shocked survivors of nuclear winter, from the shadow of the COVID-19 pandemic. The invisible aggressions in the workplace have long been present and are worsening. We're seeing it with short tempers, increasing arguments over very minor issues (the location of a trash can or the temperature of the A/C), and unjustified retaliation for imaginary slights. The list goes on and doesn't improve with expansion. We all need a moment to recover and regroup.

Actual Aggressions/Abusive Behavior

Let's see . . . I've been groped, slobbered on, pushed, and bitten. (Not by an animal and not in pre-K either!) I experienced all of this behavior in my workplace and work events, and it still does go on, even with all the guardrails, training, awareness, and social pressure.

If something like this happens to you, report or talk to someone senior about it immediately. There are no acceptable excuses for someone inflicting this kind of behavior on you. It may result in an investigation, but hopefully, you're sparing others from what you went through. In my experience, talking to the person rarely works. If you really want to leave things alone, document it in your personal notes (dated with a time stamp), try to avoid interactions with that person, and, if things remain tense, please do reconsider reporting.

Try to keep your "why" front of mind or close to front of mind so that if you're pushed in a direction you don't want to go in or a corner that's too dark, you can push back into the light. Only you and those who love you will pay the price if you don't survive your journey. I'm referring to the loss of reputation, job, opportunity, or promotion. However, I've observed countless situations over the years that led to physical harm or illness as well. Other people are often willing for you to be a casualty of their ambition; they win by hurting you. I've seen it repeatedly, and, sadly, I've lived it. The people who provoke conflict that results in horrible consequences often don't see any causation on their part, and they'll fight over the wreckage of someone's misfortunes—clients, people, and money.

During the pandemic, we saw endless cell phone videos of passengers on airplanes in mid-flight (once a fairly sacred space!) attacking their flight attendants. The incidents across all industries of actual physical violence have increased. And in the corporate world, there have been more isolated incidents. But aggressive/abusive behavior is still primarily through written or verbal communication.

Gaslighting and Other Diagnoses

One trend I've noticed in our communications, particularly post-COVID, is the tendency to talk in therapy-speak. While sometimes I confess to rolling my eyes, it can be a way to make an effective point about behavior that's difficult to classify and wasn't previously as impactful or widely discussed. And speaking solely from personal opinion and experience, people have lost their minds since the pandemic!

Gaslighting is defined in Merriam-Webster as "psychological manipulation of a person usually over an extended period of time that causes the victim to question the validity of their own thoughts, perception of reality, or memories and typically leads to confusion, loss of confidence and self-esteem . . . " It is a form of abuse, and it's more prevalent than one would imagine in corporate America. As a fun historical fact, it's also the title (*Gaslight*, actually) of a classic old movie starring Ingrid Bergman and Charles Boyer and nominated for seven Academy Awards.

The Power of Rage

Channel your rage. You read that correctly. We all have untapped rage in our lives and brains. I've found this especially true among women who haven't historically had an "acceptable" outlet for the rage.

I've also, through the process of writing this book, leaned into my rage. Yes, you heard that right—my RAGE. I didn't even know how much I was holding in. It's a rage over sixty years in the making over the restraints put on me by all the barriers to entry I've had to overcome and the things I've been required to do in the service of someone else's agenda or the outdated rules and norms of culture—both macro and micro.

If you're a soccer fan, the United States women's national soccer team (USWNT) captain, Lindsey Horan, showed us a great example of putting your rage into performance. During the 2023 World Cup, Horan had a heated altercation following a hard tackle by Netherlands star, Danielle van de Donk, despite both players being friends and teammates for the French powerhouse club, Lyon. Immediately after the altercation, Horan scored a revenge goal on Netherlands, saving the USWNT from their first World Cup game defeat in a decade, largely because of the human side of the game. Feel the rage but score the goal. Use those feelings to power you through the fear and uncertainty.

Don't turn your rage inward. It will hurt only you, and trust me, I know. Use it for good. There is so much good that can come from turning your pain into purpose. "Revenge is a dish best served cold" is an expression thought to have come from French author Eugène Sue in the 1800s. I've found that it's true. Now, I'm not encouraging you to actively pursue revenge or indulge in toxic thinking. As I said before, holding on to your rage and sense of being done wrong (when you have been) only hurts you. You need to keep your heart pure and your spirit strong. But karma is real. Stay strong and true; if you wait, you'll see that what goes around absolutely comes around. But you are not powerless. There will likely come a time when you will have the chance to even the score, and before that, you will be able to ensure that changes are made.

The Power of Words

When I was very young and occasionally bullied at school, my parents, who were very much products of their generation but wise and kind, reminded me of the old cliché, "Sticks and stones can break my bones, but words can never hurt me." They wanted me to feel empowered to fight back, to hold my head high, and stay strong. And I did and still do. However, I've long believed that words are weapons. There are many famous quotations that express this belief far more eloquently than I can, including:

"You can change the course of your life with your words." Sadly, the source of this one is said to be anonymous. I would love to know the brilliant person who basically wrote the script for my life in one sentence.

"I know nothing in this world that has as much power as a word." — Emily Dickinson[26] (or should I say the amazing and still very relevant Emily Dickinson)

"Words cannot only create emotions, they create actions. And from our actions flow the results of our lives." —Tony Robbins[27] (always thoughtful, profound, and focused on the human experience in a positive way)

Words have the power to build (or end) your career. If you're eloquent, well-spoken, and able to write well, it will take you very far. If you aren't, you can and should learn to be better (great even) at these skills. I joined a local Toastmasters group to develop my public speaking skills when I was starting out. It still exists and continues to help so many.

---

26. Emily Dickinson according to VirtuesforLife.com, "12 Quotes on the Power of Words to Encourage or Destroy," Virtues for Life, August 30, 2018. https://www.virtuesforlife.com/12-quotes-on-the-power-of-words-to-encourage-or-destroy/.

27. Tony Robbins, "Change Your Words, Change Your Life," TonyRobbins.com, accessed October 22, 2023, https://www.tonyrobbins.com/mind-meaning/change-your-words-change-your-life/.

There are also many newer ones out there you can explore. Writing classes are offered at most community colleges. These are critical skills, and I firmly believe they've contributed enormously to my overall success.

There's also a risk to writing down things, particularly with all the electronic communication. One of my clients very wisely said, "Don't put anything in writing that you wouldn't want to see on an overhead screen in front of a jury of twelve of your peers." We've all seen that play out in real time, from Watergate to *Varsity Blues* to the January 6 hearing. It's clear that our private conversations, emails, and texts can be used as blunt-force weapons. Be careful. Don't be afraid to pick up the phone or go see someone if you feel there's a problem with the job you've done, your behavior, or the relationship. You don't get to say stupid things just because you're in person or live on the phone, but it tends to produce better results when there's a conflict or an issue that can't be solved with a few emails. A positive approach vs. a potentially confrontational one is harder to recreate in a courtroom.

Conclusion

Pain, resistance, and toxic behavior can be present in the workplace. I hope that it's become more the exception than the rule; but I still see a number of problems in many of the places I go to and in many environments I'm in. We must continue to work on making our workplaces safe from fear as we all rally after surviving so much. It's on all of us, but it's mission critical for younger generations. You have the opportunity AND the power to effect major change.

Chapter 7

"And When You're High, You Never Ever Wanna Come Down"

Sometimes, the major predator to worry about when you're in a nonstop, high-stress environment isn't any of the other animals, but YOU. You may find yourself falling into unhealthy coping mechanisms or behaviors. This can have an impact on your reputation, your ability to perform, and your health. It can also create potential legal complications.

The path to a successful life includes planning how you would like to grow old and what kind of future you envision, and it's hard to focus on the long game when life is imploding. If you do succumb to substance abuse (easy to do and all of us have had our troubles with something), or if you make another high-stakes terrible decision, all your goals and plans just took a sharp left turn and have the absolute power to derail you and your future.

Substance Abuse

Right now, there's an epidemic in our country of mental illness and substance addiction, as most of us are aware. Prior to the pandemic, the substance abuse rate for executive professions hovered close to 13 percent, but post-pandemic, it's close to 20 percent.[28] And the cost and impact to everyone in all walks of life is staggering and near catastrophic. I read recently that substance abuse (alcohol and drugs) plays a major role in 50 percent of all suicides. And in the general US population, there was a 23 percent increase in alcohol abuse and a 16 percent increase in drug abuse.[29]

At different stages of our lives, our brains can change. It's now understood, based on recent scientific research, that between the ages of eighteen and twenty-five, our brains are continuing to grow, develop, and change, according to Mental Health Daily.[30] In fact, it has now been proven to be happening until our thirties. This flips everything we previously thought on its head, and it will have an impact on the way we manage and lead.

There are several things we have no control over that can determine our path and influence our lives. It's important that when we do have control, we're mindful of that and put as much effort into making the best and right decisions commensurate with the consequences. When bad things happen through pure happenstance, you should build up a set of coping skills and a support system, and be willing to do endless research. All of this allows you to regain some control and make better decisions.

28. "Hospital, Health, and Addiction Workers Group," Psychology Today, accessed October 1, 2023, https://www.psychologytoday.com/gb/contributors/maureen-oreilly-landry-phd.

29. "Hospital, Health, and Addiction Workers Group."

30. Jane C. Hu, "The Myth of the 25-Year-Old Brain," *Slate Magazine*, November 27, 2022, https://slate.com/technology/2022/11/brain-development-25-year-old-mature-myth.html.

Your First Business Trip Is a Minefield. Try Not to Let It Become a Battlefield

Going on your first business trip is absolutely a win. It demonstrates that your firm thinks you're worth an investment of time and money, and they believe you can appropriately represent your firm and company. It's a huge vote of confidence. Well done, you!

However, as with many blessings, this one can be mixed. It's a great opportunity, but it can feel like a minefield more than a series of meetings, pretty quickly.

It still feels this way to me, even after hundreds of these. When you travel, your guard is lowered. It's tiring, it's stressful, and it can involve long flights, long hours, jet lag, luggage snafus, canceled flights, hotel problems, and transportation and logistics nightmares. Let's not forget awkward moments around, but not limited to, meals, drinks, behavior, and bathroom breaks. And that's before you even worry about the behavior of your colleagues, clients, and others involved in the meetings, including office managers, personal assistants, wait staff, flight attendants, unruly passengers, and hotel staff. I have a few comfort rituals I use to keep myself centered while I'm away. It was particularly important to me when I began my insane travel schedule at around forty. That's when I realized that being willing to get on a plane to see people was a powerful tool. My son was still very young, so it wasn't without an emotional cost. I tried to do a few things that would make it a little better, including keeping my watch set to the time at home (a symbolic tie to where my heart was), limiting my away time while still accomplishing as much as I could, and resigning myself to sleeping when I'm dead.

Try to behave during a business trip with colleagues and/or clients as if your mom was watching you on a video. I know, I know, I can already hear you. For me, whose mom has been gone for over half my life, it hits a bit differently than those of you still trying to establish yourself as a fully independent and savvy adult. I do understand the cringe factor. However, I'm not saying to actually TELL your mom anything; I'm just suggesting that if you have the little voice in your head that tries to helpfully monitor your conscience and behavior, turn the volume up, waaaay up!

Attending After-Hours Events

This is my rule of thumb for all meetings, conferences, dinners, trips, or anything related to your job: like Cinderella without all the domestic drama, mice, or a fairy godmother, watch the clock. Don't wait for it to strike midnight. Eleven is plenty late enough. Just get yourself out of wherever you are, get your jammies on, take a bubble bath, watch a movie, read a book, or order hot chocolate from room service (with extra whipped cream! I mean, you are being virtuous!). Just get OUT of the bar, club, or whatever before the alcohol, drugs, or anything else appears or is fully felt. You aren't missing anything good. Please trust me on this one. I'm the queen of stealth exits or lame excuses. Take your pick. I would rather explain why I felt the need to go to my room to brush up on Kafka or wash my hair than explain why I was dancing on the table. (Although I did win a dance contest once with a client at 1:00 a.m. Still NOT a good idea. The free order of buffalo wings wasn't really life-changing, and it wasn't necessary. I just got overly enthusiastic in the way one does after a "Wow, I lost count" number of shots. Oh, and maybe there was a bottle of vodka involved. No idea. Which is a BAD idea.)

Your free will and choice will always be the first consideration. BUT. You do have to live with the consequences of a choice that leads to an unpleasant situation fueled perhaps by alcohol (or drugs), exhaustion, jet lag, or stress. In the end, the impact on you will be greater. I've had more than my fair share of self-inflicted wounds. I don't judge, truly. But I am trying to spare you pain you can avoid. Life doesn't come without pain, unfortunately. If we seek additional pain, we'll always find it. And it sucks. There are always plenty of people to tell you that you're wrong, you're unworthy, you're "bad." You're first and foremost HUMAN. We do NOT always get it right, and we often get it wrong. And we learn and grow and change. But if you don't go seeking out opportunities for self-harm and self-sabotage, it might make for a smoother ride? I personally do better when the road is smooth than when it's filled with potholes, particularly if I dug the potholes. I'm the first person to say that I've made pretty much every incredibly stupid mistake possible on the road to here, and I wish I'd chosen the easier path sometimes. Be kind to yourself when you can. We say to our children, "Make good choices today." We must do the same. And one could argue that we have better tools with which to make those good choices, but one might be out of breath.

Sex in the Office

My advice is super simple here. DON'T. NOT EVER. I DON'T CARE HOW DRUNK OR HIGH YOU ARE, HOW HOT THE OBJECT OF YOUR DESIRE IS, OR HOW ADVENTUROUS YOU ARE.

I also don't advise that you run with scissors, poke your eye out with a stick, forget to buckle your seatbelt, cross the street without looking, or jump off a cliff on a motorcycle either. PLEASE REFRAIN FROM

BEING STUPID BY SETTING YOURSELF ON FIRE. DO PUT YOUR OXYGEN MASK ON FIRST, AND PLEASE KEEP YOUR HANDS, LEGS, AND ARMS IN THE VEHICLE.

Someone once asked me in jest if I would set myself on fire to achieve my goals. I actually paused for a moment. Of course, the answer is no, but sometimes I smell smoke. Please be kind to yourself, and heed these pitfalls so you aren't lost forever in the corporate jungle without a compass or a guide.

It's an odd moment in history. And we do tend to forget that we're living history every day of our lives. We get to leave breadcrumbs and little symbols of our existence, that we were here and we mattered. But parenting is a brave new world for those of us with adult children and up to now have been measured in terms of our own benchmarks and milestones. Per the brilliant author Laurence Steinberg, PhD, it's not your imagination; things and times have changed.[31] It's not my intent to digress or open a dialogue that we don't have time for at this moment. But I do want to acknowledge that we're at an inflection point for defining what it means to be an adult, a parent, a boss, an employee, and a partner, and even down to what the new roles are by gender (or by lack of specific cultural ties or ideas based on gender).

Conclusion

My advice in this chapter has been based on personal observations and experiences collected over a long period of time. I've seen how

---

31. Martínez, A. "Psychologist Laurence Steinberg Offers Advice to Parents of Adult Children." NPR, April 11, 2023. https://www.npr.org/2023/04/11/1169194820/psychologist-laurence-steinberg-offers-advice-to-parents-of-adult-children.

you can not only be made to feel like prey, but how you can literally destroy your life. Please be kind to YOU. When you're older, you'll shudder at some of the things that did or could have occurred, and when you're enjoying a beautiful sunset or a perfect day at the beach with your children or grandchildren, I solemnly swear to you that you'll be grateful you heeded the advice.

Chapter 8

"Do You Know Where You Are?
You're in the Jungle, Baby."

It's time to take stock of what you've accomplished, what you want for the future, and how to best position yourself for it. We can miss the extraordinary or even the divine in our quest for certainty, or order, or our comfort in the mundane. Try not to miss the spectacular in your life.

Time: Your Most Precious Resource

"El tiempo es oro." ("Time Is Gold.") This Spanish saying hung on the wall in my fourth-grade classroom for reasons completely unknown.

I live by the mantra that you can buy almost anything but time, so it's one of the most precious resources any of us have. It can be stolen from you easily because we don't always place a value on it. As you get older (and aging is a privilege denied to so many), you do become more painfully aware of the clock ticking. In fact, for fun, you can go on DeathClock.com and see how many years, days, and seconds you have left to live. They would be the first to say it's only a random number generator and designed for "fun" while focusing on the fact that the clock is always ticking for all of us. I only have approximately 900 million seconds left to live, so I need to give thought to what I focus on and who I spend time with (as we all do and should, but when you're younger, you can experiment more and take some chances on people as you're learning and building your network).

Back to a golden period in literature in the sixteenth century when John Donne wrote, "Therefore, send not to know for whom the bell tolls, it tolls for thee."[32] Tick tock!

If you view your time as a precious metal or resource with the potential to earn you or cost you money, you'll make better use of it. Again, when you're younger, your time may have less commercial value, but it allows you the freedom to explore the world, spend time with all kinds of people, and try lots of different things. Don't be a miser with your time when you're young if it denies you experiences and opportunities that are priceless to you later.

What's Next? Planning for the Future

In the actual jungle, there are some safe spaces that allow the animals to rest, hide, eat, and sleep.

You might be at a watering hole or a temporary oasis.

Have an extra drink! If you've made it through the book and to a certain place in your career, you're on the path back to civilization. Or, to clarify our metaphor, we're on our way to the top of our chosen field, though there will be greater hazards ahead. But we're in a safe place to plan our future.

---

32. John Donne, "For Whom the Bell Tolls," YourDailyPoem.com, accessed October 4, 2023, https://yourdailypoem.com/listpoem.jsp?poem_id=2118.

My first question to you is, Are you happy? If the answer is yes, please proceed to the questions. If the answer is no, there's a second set of questions that follows.

If YES, you're happy:

1) Do you like what you're doing?
2) Do you see how your career is or can align with other passions and talents of yours?
3) What's your three-year, five-year, and ten-year plan?

Try to be brutally honest with yourself in your answers. The only way to find a measure of peace and happiness, large or small, is by understanding yourself. What do you really need and want? If you can see it, you can be it. Keep in touch with yourself, and reflect inward with regularity. In the end, it only matters what you think. Yes, your family counts too, but they won't be fully happy if YOU aren't.

If NO, you're not happy:

1) Would it be easy to change jobs or industries?
2) Get out your yellow notepad with the desires and obstacles. Anything on that list calling out to you now?
3) Do you need additional training to make a change?
4) What are your risks?

I consider myself a fairly ruthless pragmatist when I view my career, but I also value and embrace the power of finding your purpose and getting to a place where most days are good days. If you're unhappy, it's time to shake some things up so you can be (mostly) happy. C'mon, you GOT this. Just be honest with yourself to find your direction.

You're the only person who can answer the question of whether you're happy and satisfied with all the above. And while we're never fully either, we can get close or at least somewhat close. Depending on how many moves you've made thus far (and this is a major change from my generation, which tended to stay and stay and stay), you can quicken the pace of your achievements.

When I was starting my adventure, I found it hard to find my purpose beyond getting through the day, surviving, and not getting fired. Over time, I've been blessed to find a way to connect with my values and find a way to link my work with what I believe to be my own purpose. It's always evolving and always a work in progress, as it is for all of us for the time we're here.

I would suggest you revisit your goals on a regular basis as part of your overall strategy and hold yourself accountable.

Don't Lose Your Map! Set Goals.

I developed my own personal checklist. By thirty, I would be an account executive. And an assistant vice president by thirty-five. I would be a senior vice president at forty. Then I would be a managing director, and so on. I really was fearful (and still am, to be honest) of asking for too much. Throughout my journey, I've always been told that I'm lucky to have what I have and shouldn't rock the boat. It's never easy, and it's always a compromise. But be clear on what you want and need. At the same time, so many of the things I've been able to accomplish have had a less than 10 percent chance of ever happening, so I have forced myself to take risks and chances. Combine that with building a career in an industry to seeks to mitigate or avoid risk—the irony isn't lost on me.

There's a saying (often attributed to Woody Allen, who perhaps would know) that if you want to make God (whatever that means to you) laugh, make a plan. But I find comfort in setting, achieving, and even revisiting goals. Some of your plans, perhaps many, will change over time. It's important to take some time to sit quietly with yourself and do some serious thinking about how well your plan fits with who you are now, and we do always and often change. Sometimes we don't really notice it because it consists of microevents and challenges, seconds in a day, minutes in a week. Then a year has gone by. What we want changes and gets clearer. The most important thing you can do at this moment in your career is to be self-aware and TOTALLY honest with yourself, even to the point of emotional pain and intellectual strain.

It's worth the private pain when you're honest with yourself, and you'll find that you also have moments of joy, pride, and clarity when you train yourself to find this time and spend it in whatever way best allows you to indulge in deep thoughts—meditation, yoga, walking with or without the dog, sitting quietly in your favorite spot, listening to music, drinking tea (or something a bit stronger), playing with the cat, or birdwatching. Quiet heals your brain.

Definition of Success to YOU

I had a college course once that suggested we all write down our dreams and goals, even our stretch or pure fantasy goals for job and life.

On one side of a yellow pad (or the twenty-first-century equivalent; we're going for symbolism here), list the dreams and goals. On the other side, write down all the obstacles.

Please take a moment now to do this exercise. Grab a pad of paper (any old color will do!), a pencil, and a snack. Write out your dreams, the obstacles, and the solutions (some possible ones; it may take time to fully solve). I'll wait for you to return.

I have a helpful template if you would like one – it's part of the "Discover Your True Why" that I can send you; please see the beginning of the book for the link and QR code to grab it for free!

For example, if my dream is to play in the WNBA, the obstacles would be:

1) I'm only five foot two.
2) I have no talent for the sport whatsoever.

It's not actually one of my dreams, but if it were, I could look at other ways to be involved in supporting basketball and women's sports. A friend of mine played women's basketball in college and went on to become a super successful lawyer, so she bought a WNBA team! Now, that may not be an option, but it was a creative solution, a great investment, an opportunity to create and enhance the women's basketball community in Los Angeles and to live another version of the dream.

I wanted to be a musician and a filmmaker, as I've shared with you. Since that didn't quite work out as planned, I'm involved in the arts in other meaningful ways. This allows me to continue to feed my passion for music, film, digital content, theater, and many other interests that keep me feeling connected and present.

Find ways to keep your dreams alive, even the ones you won't get to fully achieve (then again, you may indeed land on the moon one day) or which you'll experience differently; they inspire you, feed your soul, and will bring you joy. I've dreamed of writing a book my entire life, and this is now the first step in my journey to fulfill a dream. I'm deeply honored if you're still here with me on these pages. You can always still connect to your passions and dreams.

Satisfaction

I didn't enter my industry with an intentional plan. As I shared earlier, it began as something I was doing while I finished my education and figured out my "real" career plan. I was consciously planning another life and another path while I was subconsciously planning the things I needed to do or the skills I needed to acquire to be sure I was moving forward on the road I was on. Still, I saw an opportunity to learn a profession that aligned with a number of my natural talents: working with people and building relationships; solving puzzles; doing research; incorporating my love of the arts, interest in government, and love of team building; and developing relationships with people that either turn into friendships or at least years of respectful collaboration.

One of the things I'm proudest of is the fact that I believe you'll like me better ten years from now than today. I'm willing to put in the work to foster a friendship that's mutually beneficial and real. I want to know your "why" and help you accomplish things that support that. I want to be a better person, and I'm grateful to you for helping me do and become that. Those qualities all helped me craft a career out of whole cloth and fairy dust, so to speak. I needed to figure out a path forward with the options available to me with the hand I was dealt.

This is where you start. Where you go, what you achieve, and where you finish will be largely on you and how you run your race. I hope my experiences above have given you some ideas for your own plan and your own successes. (And I know there will be many—practicing believing now!) Please feel free to use any of my tools or lessons at will. I hope I've served you well as a guide.

Don't forget to stop for water, reload your "weapons," and rest when you can. Life can present unwelcome obstacles or challenges, but it can also offer spontaneous moments of beauty and joy. Your imaginary glass can be half-full, half-empty, or overflowing. You can't always control it; you don't always get to have a say, even when you deserve it or, by any reasonable viewpoint, should absolutely have input. But you still have the ultimate choice to be a victim, survivor, hero (even if it's only to one person), or zero. Pay attention, focus, work hard, play hard, and believe.

Congratulations and have a drink, smoothie, or a cookie on me!! It's time to celebrate—if only for a moment. You've made it to the center of the jungle, a powerful place. I am with you in spirit, toasting you or covered in chocolate chips. Take a deep breath, grab a snack, and ponder your future and next steps. You've done it. Keep doing it, stay the course, and keep the faith. I know YOU have GOT this!

Most importantly, you're alive. You've eluded the hungry lion, angry hyenas, charging rhinos, ornery orangutans, and those deceiving hippos. (Fun fact: Hippos are the deadliest large land animals on the planet. Despite a common view of them as cartoon animals in a tutu, they're very aggressive. Their weight alone could crush you—2,750 kg on average). Curiously, on my 2015 safari, staying by a riverbank near a colony of hippos, I learned that they love to "sing" noisily—all night.

"If there's ever a tomorrow when we're not together, there's something you must always remember:

"You are braver than you believe,

Stronger than you seem,

And smarter than you think.

But the most important thing is,

Even if we're apart,

I'll always be with you."

—Carter Crocker, *Pooh's Grand Adventure: The Search for Christopher Robin*

Acknowledgments

To my Big Idea to Bestseller family:

Jake Kelfer: Reading your book changed my life. Thank you for your leadership, vision, and inspiration for all of us—changing the world one book at a time!

Cory Hott: Without your friendship, creativity, and support, there would be no book.

Mary-Theresa Tringale: You empowered and supported me, answered all my inane questions, gave me amazing guidance, and dragged me over the finish line—thank you, this book belongs to you too.

Catt Editing: Thank you sooo much!! Your editing was truly a rare and precious gift.

To the amazing female friends and leaders who have helped and inspired me: Gwen Abbott, Holly Bauer, Dr. Jill Biden, LeeAnn Black, Kim Carnow, Carla Christofferson, Secretary Hillary Rodham Clinton, Sylvia Mendoza Driebe, Sonnie Faires, Kaia Ferari-Munoz, Nancy Gannon, Nicole Hefferan, Aileen Jauffret, Dina Johnson, Jenn Jeonghwa Kang, Lena Kennedy, Kara MacDonald, Claudia Mandato, Sandie Matsuura, Bari Mattes, Lynda Meyer, Leslie Miller, Guillermina

Molina, Liz Hirsh Naftali, Krista Newkirk, Michelle Obama, Linda O'Hanlon, Karen Reich, Deborah Rutter, Annette Sciallo, Amy Singh, Jaynie Studenmund, Governor Gretchen Whitmer.

To the amazing male friends and leaders who have helped and inspired me: Congressman Peter Aguilar, President Joe Biden, Austin Beutner, Senator Cory Booker, William Harold Borthwick, Brad Butwin, Martin Checov, Dennis Cheng, President William J. Clinton, Robert Davidson, Phil Doolittle, James Ellis, Geoff Garrett, Guy Halgren, Dana Kopper, Bob Kresge, Dr. Koroush Maddahi, Marc Maister, Ambassador Noah Mamet, Jim Messina, Henry Munoz, Governor Gavin Newsom, Tim Noonan, President Barack Obama, Adrian Pietrariu, Charlie Plowman, David Rubenstein, Luca Salvi, John Stoia, George Strong, Jonathan Weedman, J.C. Wileman

To my best friend of fifty years, Linda Kresge, for sharing the safaris and saving my life too many times to count. And in memory of her wonderful parents, Jim and Keiko Jinks who loved me as a second daughter. To my own parents, Mike and Nell Hostovich, I miss you every day, and I hope I have made your proud of me. Doug and Michael, you are my heart.

Dear Reader:

I am so honored that you chose to read my book and gave me the precious gift of your time. I hope I have helped you, even in some small way.

I would like to ask you a huge additional favor. It would mean the world to me if you would take a moment to leave a review on Amazon. Thank you so much for your consideration of this request!

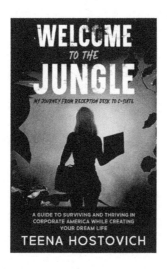

About Teena

 **Teena Hostovich** is the Vice Chair, Pacific, of Lockton Insurance, based in Los Angeles. She has combined her lifelong passion for the arts, history, and education with her corporate responsibilities, political activism, and philanthropic work. She is a member of the Clinton Global Initiative and the White House Historical Association. President Biden recently appointed her to the President's Advisory Committee for the Arts, and she is the Co-Chair of the Advisory Council to the Kennedy Center's President and Chairman. She is on the boards of the LA Philharmonic, the USC Marshall School of Business (her alma mater), the University of Redlands, the National Advisory Council for the American Film Institute, and an advisor for the Women's Studies Programs at Oxford University and UVA. In 2022, she was on the Steering Committee for Prop 28 Vote Arts and Music in California Schools which passed overwhelmingly and now provides funding for arts education to all California public school children.

Teena lives in La Canada, CA, with her husband, Doug Martinet. Her son, Michael Martinet, is at USC.